WHAT BUSINESS WANTS FROM HIGHER EDUCATION

Diana G. Oblinger
Anne-Lee Verville

AMERICAN COUNCIL ON EDUCATION ★
ORYX PRESS ★
Series on Higher Education
1998

The rare Arabian Oryx is believed to have inspired the myth of the unicorn. This desert antelope became virtually extinct in the early 1960s. At that time several groups of international conservationists arranged to have 9 animals sent to the Phoenix Zoo to be the nucleus of a captive breeding herd. Today the Oryx population is over 1,000 and over 500 have been returned to the Middle East.

© 1998 by The Oryx Press
4041 North Central at Indian School Road
Phoenix, Arizona 85012-3397

Published simultaneously in Canada
Printed and Bound in the United States of America

∞ The paper used in this publication meets the minimum requirements of American National Standard for Information Science—Permanence of Paper for Printed Library Materials, ANSI Z39.48, 1984.

Library of Congress Cataloging-in-Publication Data

Oblinger, Diana.
    What business wants from higher education / Diana G. Oblinger, Anne-Lee Verville.
        p. cm.—(American Council on Education/Oryx Press series on higher education)
    Includes bibliographical references (p. 165) and index (p. 175).
    ISBN 1-57356-206-8 (alk. paper)
    1. Industry and education—United States.   2. Education, Higher—Economic aspects—United States.   3. Organizational change—United States.   I. Verville, Anne-Lee.   II. Title.   III. Series.
LC1085.2.035   1998
378'.01—dc21   98-14889
                                                                            CIP

CONTENTS

FOREWORD

T he rising importance of higher education to the economic viability of nations as well as individuals clearly stands as one of the great pressures driving reflection and change within American colleges and universities. As our nation leads the world economy from the industrial revolution into the knowledge revolution, institutions of higher education are being viewed as major *economic* resources—generators of *productive* capacities in their own right—to an extent never before witnessed. As Peter Drucker (1994) notes, the world economy in which the United States must compete is rapidly evolving to the point where knowledge is the primary source of comparative economic advantage among companies and countries. Advantages in terms of land, labor, and capital that once determined economic prosperity are receding in importance relative to the advantage of knowing how to put those resources to the most productive purposes at the least cost. According to Drucker, the effects of this shift will likely be all-pervading:

> In fact, the acquisition and distribution of formal knowledge may come to occupy the place in the politics of the knowledge society which the acquisition and distribution of property and income have occupied in our politics over the two or three centuries that we have come to call the Age of Capitalism. (Drucker 1994, 66)

The speed of change has become a defining characteristic of the knowledge age. In this new knowledge-based economy, colleges and universities have a unique responsibility for developing and maintaining the knowledge resources that now form the foundation of our economic growth. As institutions dedicated to education, research, and public service, they are driven to this responsibility not only by higher education's historic mission but also by the growing importance of that mission in the new world context.

In confronting the level of change required by the globalization of economic competition and ever-increasing advances in information technology, American businesses and corporations have had to radically restructure themselves to survive and thrive in the global knowledge economy. As they have adapted, their workforce needs and requirements have changed as well. Because of the importance of education to their competitive success, they are evaluating ever more critically whether college and university graduates are meeting their needs. Mid-level managers, CEOs, and human resources professionals consistently state that they need college graduates who are

- able to think critically and communicate effectively, both verbally and in writing;
- comfortable working in teams, both within their areas and cross-functionally;
- proficient in information and telecommunications technologies; and
- knowledgeable about the global environment in which they must function and facile in the cultural diversity it entails.

The fear within businesses is that the "ivory tower" may not be sufficiently sensitive to the educational implications of the rapid pace of change. While the business community has endured wave after wave of consolidations, downsizings, reorganizations, and changes in basic management philosophies and organizational cultures, it has witnessed little recognition of these new realities by colleges and universities. With the rise of corporate universities and for-profit institutions, traditional colleges and universities may find their dominant position as the provider of higher education under increasing challenge.

No one is advocating that colleges and universities should become training institutes. The broader educational purposes of higher education—including the development of a well-educated society with the flexibility and tolerance that derive from a broad understanding of our society's history, traditions, and multicultural roots—remain the central focus. In fact, one of the greatest challenges facing higher education leaders is to articulate clearly and persuasively the extent to which the skills and abilities that businesses say they need from college graduates already are developed through the traditional arts and sciences. However, colleges and universities must accelerate the pace of curricula restructuring to expand the flexible interactive modes of teaching and learning that are sought by the workforce and made possible by the technology revolution. A convergence exists between the new demands and expectations of workers for learning and creating with the new capabilities of information and communications technology to enhance the educational process. Colleges and universities must capitalize on this convergence to offer faculty and students new opportunities for teaching and learning. Moreover, higher education must stand ready to measure institutional performance in terms of the demonstrated learning of our students, particularly in the areas deemed relevant by prospective employers. These are essential dimensions for change within higher education if we are to attain our full potential for sustaining and enhancing the foundations of our knowledge-based economy.

These key steps in the evolution of higher education may be facilitated by working in partnership with business and industry to identify and pursue significant issues and methods for change. Direct conversations between corporate and business leaders and their counterparts in higher education, as well as the direct participation of business leaders in the evaluation and restructuring efforts of colleges and universities, may provide the higher education community with the external perspectives and insights that can contribute to truly constructive change within the academy. Together, the business and higher education communities can ensure that America's college and university graduates are prepared to pursue fulfilling lives and careers in the globally competitive and technologically networked environment that awaits them.

Molly Corbett Broad, president, The University of North Carolina System

PREFACE

Our motivation for writing this book is the pace of change. It has never been faster. It seems as though neither organizations nor people can move fast enough to stay ahead of the changes brought about by globalization and technology. Both business and higher education will be challenged to stay abreast of these changes. Our hope is that if the academy better understands what business needs from the graduates of colleges and universities, higher education will help business and society by better preparing them for these waves of change.

There will be multiple challenges. How do we effectively lead change? How do we prepare a workforce for the information age? What will business need in employees five years from now that is different from what is needed today? In 10 years? How do we simultaneously make education more individualized and personalized while ensuring students obtain a global, holistic perspective? How do we create perpetual learning organizations?

As competition grows all around us, businesses constantly wonder how to sustain a winning course and speed. Higher education can be the all-important differentiator because the quality of graduates forms the core competitive advantage for business. The point is not that the past is wrong or that education is failing; the point is that the future will be different. Facts taught in isolation and individual competitiveness will not prepare today's or tomorrow's workforce for the pressures our businesses face. Neither will all training and no education or all technology and no humanities make individuals ready for the future. We will need a mixture of timeliness and timelessness in the curricula if business is to redefine itself and its success in a global, interdependent society.

The purpose of this book is to help our colleagues in higher education and business understand the dramatic changes taking place around us and how these will affect the workplace and education. We believe that education will make a critical difference in how our society deals with change. Unfortunately, change is not a topic with which many of us are comfortable. Most people prefer to talk about change rather than to welcome it or take action to shape it.

Because of the tight association between education and economic competitiveness, social stability and personal well-being, business is deeply concerned about what happens in our colleges and universities. Being concerned with education is not synonymous with saying that we are telling higher education what to teach or how to manage the organization. However, for education to help meet the needs of business, there must be a dialog between business and higher education.

As the American Council on Education (ACE) found in their 1997 study, "A chasm separates the academic and corporate worlds. Corporate leaders are convinced that university employees—including administrators and faculty members—do not understand the requirements of the private sector and the need for students to be better prepared for the demands of a changing global economy. Academic leaders are equally sure that corporations have little respect for the campus and that U.S. universities are, in fact, world class. Recently employed alumni value their college experiences but report that they had too little direction and guidance in choosing and preparing for a career" (ACE 1997, 3).

We hope this book will stimulate a dialog between the business and academic communities that will result in actions that better prepare students for life and the world of work. To do that, in the first chapter we have shared with you a description of how business is transforming itself from a rigid hierarchy into a "flexible organization," allowing it to adapt rapidly as the environment continues to change. The second chapter describes the significant value that higher education adds to individuals and communities. We believe a joint dialog can enhance this strong historic base. Of course, changing once won't be enough. The next three chapters describe how shifts in demographics, technology, and globalization will continue to change our lives and businesses. At the end of each chapter we have suggested a list of "questions to ask" to stimulate dialog and self-examination.

With an understanding of this changing environment, chapter 6 describes what business needs from graduates and education. The employees of the future will be different from those of the past. The next chapter focuses on the learning environment, which will need to change if students are to be prepared for the problem-solving, team-based, ambiguous workplace of today and tomorrow. Chapter 8 describes how the academy can have an impact on K–12 education, resulting in better preparation of those workers who do not enter postsecondary institutions as well as those who enroll in higher education. We believe we can improve upon our traditional system of K–12 and higher education using what we know about cognition, communications, and computing.

It would be impossible to write a prescription for precisely what higher education should do. Institutions are unique. Situations differ. However, there are some common philosophies that we believe can be applied to improve education, such as ensuring that learning is the core value of the institution; creating an enlightened organization where finance, governance, and policy help instead of hinder change; and developing the attitude of welcoming change. The final three chapters focus on these philosophies. Our experiences and those of our colleagues and other experts tell us that the pace of change will never be slower than it is today. We must learn to welcome change, not fear it.

We would like to thank those who shared their insight with us, particularly Bob Jones of the National Alliance of Business and the 1997 class of Leadership California. Thanks go to our IBM colleagues, as well, especially Lawrence Bivins, Jack Canavan, Jim Cortada, Jim Ferrell, Jill Kanin-Lovers, Larry Prusak, Bill Pulleyblank, and Kathy Walsh.

We hope this book will stimulate a dialog within higher education, but also one that encompasses business and government. We all stand to gain—or lose—by the actions we take to prepare for the future.

ACKNOWLEDGMENTS

I would like to thank Adam, Brian, Chris, and Andrew for teaching me to welcome change. Their thirst for knowledge and their ease with technology, creativity, and energy provide me with a source of motivation and pride. I would like to particularly thank my husband, Jim, for his encouragement and support, and for keeping me focused on the things that really matter.

Diana Oblinger

I want to especially thank my colleague Diana Oblinger who has shouldered so much of the work of this book. My thanks also go to all the IBM colleagues who have supported me through the years and allowed me to spend time with our customers. Finally, my thanks go to our education customers for their confidence in our outstanding IBM education team.

Anne-Lee Verville

The proceeds of this book are being contributed to the IBM Foundation for support of scholarships to qualified students.

PART ONE

· · · · · · · · · · · ·

Life as We Know It

CHAPTER 1

The Flexible Organization

A merican business has experienced a transformation in the past decade that dwarfs the changes brought about by the industrial revolution. Today's corporation is leaner and more productive, flatter and less hierarchical. It focuses relentlessly on quality and customer satisfaction. Global competition as well as the challenges and opportunities offered by technology are forcing businesses to rethink their strategies and operating structures. Although many corporations restructured during the 1980s and 1990s, they will have to restructure again. Business can expect to face new, potentially more vigorous economic competition in the years ahead (ACE 1997). Most of the changes in the work environment during the 1990s have been motivated by the need for flexibility and adaptability so businesses can respond to new opportunities or threats. The goal has been to create the "flexible organization."

In fact, the "organization" may be a facade. Just beyond the surface is a collection of groups and subgroups linked together in an intricate web where value, goods, services, and ideas are interchanged. The mission of these decentralized groups has shifted from *high-volume* production of standard commodities to *high-value* goods and services (Reich 1991).

Speed and agility are so important that these high-value firms are often not weighted down with large overhead costs such as office buildings, plants, equipment, and payroll. They must be able to switch directions quickly, pursue options when they arise, discover new linkages between problems and solutions — wherever they may lie. Office space, factories, and warehouses can be rented; standard equipment can be leased; common components can be bought wholesale; secretaries, data processors, bookkeepers, and routine production workers can be hired temporarily. Instead of looking like a pyramid with a chief executive officer (CEO) at the top and hourly workers at the base, today's corporation more closely resembles a web.

To be in the high-value business, firms need problem solvers, problem identifiers, and strategic brokers.

- Problem-solving skills allow employees to put things together in unique ways (whether they are alloys, molecules, semiconductor chips, software code, pension portfolios, or information). These people are involved in a continuing search for new applications, combinations, and refinements capable of solving emerging problems.
- Problem identifiers help customers understand their needs and how those needs can best be met by customized products. In contrast to traditional marketing and sales, these problem identifiers must have an intimate knowledge of a customer's business.
- Strategic brokers link problem solvers with problem identifiers—they continuously engage in managing ideas. These people understand enough about technologies and markets to see the potential for new products, raise the money necessary to launch projects, and assemble the right teams to carry them out (Reich 1991).

Are today's higher education students prepared for this environment of speed, agility, and flexibility? Are they adept at being problem solvers, problem identifiers, or strategic brokers? Not well enough, according to many experts. "New hires have little understanding of the role of the corporation. They do not have the flexibility required to function effectively in it. And they lack the critical skills: listening, communicating, defining problems, leveraging the skills of others in teams, and functioning effectively in an ambiguous, complex and rapidly changing environment" (ACE 1996, 8).

Changes occurring in the business environment are leading to more complex, flexible, and responsive organizations. More than ever, business relies on higher education to prepare students for this rapidly changing environment.

NEW RULES

Since 1970, American corporations have laid off millions of employees. Layoffs initially affected hourly workers and supervisors in manufacturing and other industries in the "rust belt." More recently they have extended into the ranks of managers and executives in the banking, finance, service, and high-technology industries—the jobs thought to be the foundation for the twenty-first century (ACE 1997).

Reengineering is the order of the day. Organizations are leaner; managers provide less direction and give employees more decision-making responsibility as well as more accountability. Work is accomplished by teams, not just by individuals. Increasingly, business is based on a new set of rules. Predicting the future based on the past no longer works.

The practices of many "winners" fall outside the norm. Particularly in technology-related businesses, new rules are emerging. In many respects it would be fair to say that there are two kinds of companies in the information age economy: the quick and the dead. Internet time limits product adoption "windows of opportunity" to 18–24 months. Survival demands rapid product life cycles. One way to speed product innovation is to continually render your own products obsolete through replacement or renovation. If you don't, someone else will.

Marketing is no longer to the masses. Mass advertising, mass merchandising, and mass assembly-line manufacturing are outdated strategies. Winning products target a specific community. Marketeers think in terms of how to personalize, individualize, and customize; i.e., how to deal with markets-of-one. Winners distinguish themselves through customization so that their products, services, and ideas stand out (Lewis 1996).

In fact, classical economics (supply equals demand) may no longer apply to many of these markets. Survival in today's economy is often based on non-linear, mathematical chaos–based principles. With value webs (interconnected groups of suppliers, aggregators, value-added remarketers, consumers, etc.) flux is constant; suppliers become consumers, competitors become collaborators, and so on. Although differentiation may occur at almost any point in the value web, sustainable competitive advantage belongs only to those whose innovations buyers value.

Whether the new rules of business apply to all organizations or not, we have witnessed a changing dynamic: the old rules of size and stability are being displaced by speed and flexibility. This complexity is changing the nature of work and workers. As Reich (1991, 196) asserts, "The economic well-being of Americans no longer depends on the profitability of the corporations they own, or on the prowess of their industries, but on the value they add to the global economy through their skills and insights. Increasingly, it is the jobs that Americans do, rather than the success of abstract entities like corporations, industries or national economies that determine their standard of living."

THE CHANGING WORKFORCE

Not only are organizations and the nature of work changing, the workforce is changing. These shifts will dramatically change the composition and age distribution of the labor force by 2005. At the same time they will change the composition and age distribution for higher education.

- In 1990, European Americans accounted for 78 percent of the U.S. civilian labor force. In the same year, African Americans accounted for 11 percent of the labor force; Latin Americans 8 percent; and Asian Americans the remaining 3 percent. By 2005, however, demographic shifts will reshape the American labor force. Minorities will capture a larger share of the jobs, while the percentage of European-American workers will fall to 73 percent of the total.
- By 2000, new hires in the United States will come from an applicant pool that is 85 percent minority, female, or immigrant.
- By 2005, the number of Latin-American workers will virtually equal the number of African-American workers, while Asian-American workers will constitute 4 percent of the labor force (Fisher 1990).

The labor pool will also change its age characteristics.

- In 1975, workers 16–34 years old comprised nearly half of the U.S. civilian labor force. By 2005, however, this age cohort will be eclipsed by the 35–55-year-old cohort, which will account for 48 percent of the labor force.
- The aging labor force will require new investments by the public and private sectors in education and training to facilitate economic growth and productivity.
- As older adults work longer and postpone retirement, many seek continuing education to stay abreast of new technologies and developments within professional disciplines. Among those who do retire, many take advantage of enrichment education, pursuing areas of interest they have not had the time or money to explore previously.

In addition, more immigrants with professional credentials are being admitted to the United States. In 1989, more than 1 million immigrants were granted admission to the United States—an increase of 106 percent over 1980. Of those admitted, slightly more than half were given preference because they were classified as "professional or highly skilled." Predictions are for this trend to continue (University Continuing Education Association 1992).

The U.S. workforce has become more educated. Since 1970, the portion of the labor pool with more than a high school diploma has more than doubled.

| Share of Civilian Labor Force | | |
High School Dropout	High School Graduate	Postsecondary Education
1970	36%	38%	26%
1980	21	40	39
1996	11	33	56

Source: National Association of Business (NAB). 1997e. The multifaceted returns to education. <http://www.nab.com/econ/returntoed.html>.

The adult population of the United States has never had more formal education. Nationally, more than 75 percent of adults have earned high school diplomas or have passed the General Educational Development (GED) exam; almost 25 percent have attended one to three years of college; and over 20 percent have a four-year or higher degree (Marks 1996).

Consider three implications of these trends for higher education.

1. As more employees stay in the workforce for additional years, the demands for training, education, and retraining will increase.
2. As the labor pool becomes increasingly diverse, that diversity should be mirrored in the college-going population. With tuition continuing to move beyond the means of many families, either pressure on public institutions will intensify or tuition discounting will become even more prevalent if diversity is to be appropriately reflected in colleges and universities.
3. The educational experience of an increasing proportion of the working population is less than positive. How will the educational "establishment" successfully train those who feel that the "system" failed them?

THE CHANGING NATURE OF WORK AND WORKERS

Throughout society, science and technology are priorities. The rationale is straightforward: science and technology fuel growth. Although they make many aspects of our lives better, just about everything has become more complex.

Professionals and Technicians

One result of this increase in science and technology is that the nature of work and the requirements of workers are changing. In contrast with 50 years ago, there are few workers who are not asked to make decisions and solve problems. The notion of white-collar/blue-collar workers is an artifact of an industrial age model where decision making was thought to be the work of executives,

requiring both a college degree and work experience. Workers in a scientifi-
cally and technologically intensive society are more appropriately described as
"professionals" and "technicians" than as white-collar and blue-collar workers.

Professionals

The term *professional* has traditionally been used to signify someone who has
either graduated from a "professional" school (e.g., law, medicine) or someone
who has mastered a body of knowledge. In the mid-century economy a
"professional" was one who had mastered a particular domain of knowledge.
The knowledge existed in advance, ready to be mastered. It had been
recorded in dusty tomes or codified with precise rules and formulas. Once the
novice had dutifully absorbed the knowledge and had passed an examination
attesting to its absorption, professional status was conferred—usually through
a ceremony of appropriately medieval pageantry and costume (Reich 1991).

A more relevant definition of a professional today is someone with the
ability to accomplish complicated tasks or someone who has complex knowledge (Prusak 1997a). These skills are not necessarily based on mastering a
specific or documented body of knowledge. Many professions are not available
as majors in college. Being a commodities broker, a product manager, or a
systems integrator entails complicated tasks. The mastery of specific practices,
heuristics, information, and tacit knowledge are required. In addition, a
significant amount of preparation for the profession is based on "learning by
doing." Nonetheless, the professional will likely have an advanced degree,
have participated in some type of an apprenticeship, and will certainly work as
a member of a team.

The activities of professionals include sales, analysis, synthesis, and judgment. Professionals produce intangible outputs. They engage in symbolic
analysis services which include problem identification, problem solving, and
problem brokering. This work is done by "turning reality into abstract images
that can be rearranged, juggled, experimented with, communicated to other
specialists and then transformed into reality" (Reich 1991, 178). Many of
these people call themselves research scientists, software engineers, civil
engineers, public relations executives, investment bankers, lawyers, real estate
developers, management consultants, financial consultants, management information specialists, strategic planners, and systems analysts. The tools that
professionals use to manipulate symbols—data, words, oral and visual representations—are information technology (IT) tools. Education—throughout
life—is critical to professionals.

Technicians

The other category of worker that is growing rapidly is that of the *technician*. Technicians are those who handle the complex data, software, techniques, and processes that support our production systems ranging from production lines to distribution to maintenance.

Technicians, like professionals, are heavily involved with IT in their work; however, their jobs are more dependent on technology and techniques than on analysis. While a technician must master a body of practice, it is less complex and more physical than that of the professional. Think of it as the difference between understanding how to repair a photocopy machine (technician) and designing one (professional). Although a large portion of technicians take two- or four-year degrees, much of the knowledge and many of the tasks are learned on the job (Prusak 1997a). Even so, the foundation provided by education in terms of skills, such as problem solving and interpersonal communication, are essential.

Growing Complexity of Work

Many factors contribute to work becoming more complex. More technology is used in the workplace. More technology is involved in products. The people with whom we interact are more diverse in terms of culture, gender, ethnicity, and age, making interpersonal communication more complicated. As layers of middle management are removed for the sake of efficiency, different tasks are being required of workers. All these factors add to the complexity of work.

The more complex a process or an event, the less likely it is that a single individual can master it. Complexity also compounds the likelihood that something will "go wrong" and specialized knowledge will be required to correct it. For example, few of us would consider trying to repair a car anymore. The dozens of microprocessors and finely tuned instruments require specialized skill and electronic monitoring. The knowledge needed in these complex situations will most likely be found in groups of professionals or technicians. To be efficient and effective, organizations must gain access to this non-articulated knowledge. Some organizations depend on luck to access it. Others are creating processes to identify and consolidate knowledge (Prusak 1997a).

Intangible outcomes

For many businesses, their identity is embodied in characteristics such as customer service, innovation, quality, brand loyalty, or reputation. These are intangible qualities. Across multiple industries, service and manufacturing are blending. *Fortune* magazine merged the *Fortune 500* manufacturing list with the *Fortune 500* service list a few years ago, anecdotal evidence of the blurring of the distinction. A more significant trend is that actual manufacturing and production operations are becoming more knowledge intensive. Knowledge—an intangible—is a key ingredient in the success of a tangible product.

Reich (1991) defines a new type of worker—the symbolic analyst—who specializes in intangible outcomes. Research scientists create hypothetical molecules designed for their pharmacological properties, which are tested first in simulated environments. Real estate developers conceptualize and market ambience that may ultimately be transformed into a physical place. Financial analysts compare portfolios simulating earning scenarios for clients. Knowledge is a key component in each of these intangible products.

Workplace knowledge

A firm's competitive advantage depends more than anything on its knowledge. It depends on what the firm knows, how it uses what it knows, and how fast it can know something new. For example, product innovations are the result of a group's knowledge of unserved markets and/or new technical possibilities; efficient operations come from shared knowledge of how things work and how they could work; market share grows with better knowledge of customers and of how to serve them (Prusak 1997b).

As work itself changes, there is much greater emphasis on workplace knowledge. Knowledge can be defined as the collection of experiences, heuristics, values, and cognitive frameworks that are embodied in individuals. Over time, this knowledge becomes embedded within the routines, processes, and norms of the organization. As the knowledge of individuals is captured within the system, the organization "learns." Learning organizations are organizations that are skilled at creating, acquiring, and transferring knowledge. They also reflect that new knowledge in unique insight or through modified behavior.

Senior executives are recognizing that knowledge and learning represent the preeminent source of sustainable advantage in a fast-moving, highly competitive world. They know it is no longer enough to leave critical knowledge sitting passively in the minds of individual employees. Workforce mobility, falling educational standards, and the rapid rate of business change mean that individuals can no longer be relied upon to provide consistent, comprehensive insight. Instead, the knowledge trapped within the employee base must be leveraged to the organizational level, where it can be accessed, synthesized, augmented, and deployed for the benefit of all. Yesterday's informal or tacit knowledge management techniques—the desktop, the hallway conversation, the memo, the trade show—are no longer sufficient in a period of radical change (Prusak 1997b).

Knowledge and networks

Computing is spreading throughout the workplace. This phenomenon will continue as computers and applications become cheaper, faster, smaller, and easier to use. One primary use of the computer is as a communicator—seeking out knowledge and information—without necessarily housing or producing the information. This communication role accounts for the spectacular growth of intranets and the Internet. The modern, wired desktop, which is tied to internal networks and the Internet, is an attempt to cope with the complex demands of the workplace. Either internally or externally, workers can seek out knowledgeable peers or experts and information to fulfill their knowledge needs.

Information technology has become essential to workplace knowledge. What is different is that today IT is transparent to the user, ubiquitous, and more capable than ever of capturing knowledge, as opposed to mere data or words. Real, interactive networks are made possible by telecommunications and technologies like groupware, and can put knowledgeable people—who could never find one another before—in touch with each other. As these technologies become richer in their means of expression (through the integration of multiple media), computers will take on an even greater role in enabling the use of knowledge as a transforming agent (Prusak 1997b).

The importance of workplace knowledge has changed the function, role, and importance of networks within a business. "The need to manage knowledge actively becomes more obvious when what you sell is knowledge. For a research lab, a consulting firm, a software vendor not to manage knowledge would be equivalent to Wal-Mart not managing inventory or Ford not managing production" (Prusak 1997b, xi).

As workplace knowledge increases in importance, employees increase their search for knowledge, offer their knowledge to others, and broker knowledge within, as well as outside, the firm. These activities establish knowledge "markets" where knowledge buyers and sellers can exchange their "goods" at a fair price. The "price" is often some form of reciprocity.

This knowledge "market" is vibrant and growing rapidly. Groups, teams, communities of practice, and other informal groups become involved in how knowledge is created, used, and distributed. These knowledge networks do related work, share context, vocabulary, and goals. They often exist across functions, across time and space, and sometimes across firms themselves (Prusak 1997a).

WORKPLACE LANDSCAPE

Science and technology have unquestionably changed the workplace. The changing dynamics of business are reflected in the work environment as well as in the behavior required of employees. Complexity, speed, and mobility characterize today's workplace. As the workplace changes, so will organizations and the behaviors sought in employees. At least in part, these behaviors will derive from an education that encourages observation, exploration, analysis, decision making, and communication. Among the most important behaviors in the future is the capacity for lifelong learning.

Complexity

Mergers, alliances, and new companies

Huge corporations are coming together; household names are disappearing. More than half of the companies on the *Fortune 500* list of the largest companies 20 years ago no longer exist. Mergers, alliances, and new companies spring up, seemingly overnight, to capitalize on a marketplace based on individual choice and mass customization of products.

Being able to identify the niche and describe what is needed to fill it is a complex skill requiring detailed understanding of the customer, the marketplace, and the product or process involved. Customization is often based on demographics. More and more firms are specializing in products or services for African Americans, Latin Americans, or other specialized interest groups. Regional differences are being recognized by McDonald's and other consumer companies. As targeted marketing increases, there will be additional emphasis on aggregators, as well. These are companies that aggregate or collect products and services for delivery in a form the customers want at a price they are willing to pay. If you are a fly fisherman, your aggregator may send you a catalog (or host a Web site) with all the rods, flies, classes, excursions, videos, and clothes you will ever need.

Globalization

China, India, Eastern Europe, and the other emerging markets account for more than 25 percent of the total items bought and sold in the industrialized world. Within the next 10 years, emerging markets could account for 50 percent. The pace of change in global competition is striking. Consider that from the beginning of our industrial revolution, it took the United States 47 years to double its gross domestic product, per capita. Japan's doubled in 34 years, China's in 10 years.

As companies position themselves to expand within the global economy, their efforts are often stultified by deficiencies of knowledge. Their people simply do not know enough about how to spot global opportunities, or once an opportunity is spotted, how business is done in that part of the world. Worse yet, they may not understand the basic model by which the business succeeds, or how to replicate that success in new outposts (Prusak 1997b). Globalization has made work more complex.

Another source of complexity related to globalization is that people work together without being in the same country. Increasingly, detailed plans and projects are being developed by geographically dispersed teams through sharing computer files, videoconferencing, and whiteboards. Software is developed by moving successive iterations of code from the United States to India to Europe in one 24-hour time frame. Jobs in the same company will be scattered throughout the world with orders handled in one location, accounting in another, and production yet somewhere else.

Dealing with ambiguity

As the environment gets more complex, ambiguity becomes greater. Yet dealing with ambiguity—at all levels—is important to success. Consider quality, for example. First, quality is perceived. It is based on the customer's judgment, not one's own. Second, the quality of the product is important, but most competitive situations will be won or lost on the quality of the services that are associated with the product rather than the product itself. Third, quality is relative and not absolute. It is measured against one's competitors and can change rapidly (IBM 1990). The emphasis on quality, services, and customers emphasizes the importance of the front line and the ambiguity with which employees increasingly cope. One of the biggest changes in the high-tech workplace is the greater role that front-line workers are playing—initiating and implementing strategies to improve bottom-line performance. Many of their roles are undefined and ambiguous.

Reduced supervision

Another source of complexity is the reduction in direction and supervision provided to employees. Many managers are supervising more employees. Matrix management is commonplace. Within teams that may be comprised of individuals from several units and different geographies, who supervises whom? Employees may be "supervised" on a daily basis by a team leader rather than their own line manager. How does one manage employees who are "remote," that is, those who live hundreds or thousands of miles away? It is common for managers to be responsible for a dozen employees, yet those individuals are located in as many different cities. Others manage employees who telecommute. Working with, managing, and evaluating people one rarely sees face-to-face is a much more complex task than when physically working with those individuals on a daily basis.

Multiple management styles

Business and industry have also recognized that a single management style will not work with all employees. Supervisors are responsible for people with different motivations, styles, and levels of responsibility; therefore, manage-

ment becomes more situational than by the book. Replacing the old com-
mand-and-control type of management, coaching has become the dominant
mantra. Another trend that adds to complexity is that management is less
focused on day-to-day activities and more on the broader development of the
business and the individual.

Working in an outsourcing environment raises new management challenges, as well. Employers may not be allowed to provide direct supervision to
contract employees, due to Internal Revenue Service (IRS) regulations. How
does one manage or work with people when one cannot give instructions,
feedback, or rewards? Managing in this environment presents a new kind of
interpersonal skill, one in which few managers are trained.

Mobility

Physical mobility

Last year, more than 30 million people worked from home offices. At IBM, for
example, 25 percent of the North American workforce is "mobile," i.e., they
telecommute or work from home offices. Many companies have significantly
reduced their costs of real estate and related expenses through telecommuting.
Cost savings benefit stockholders. Employees are better able to balance work
and personal lives, and to spend their time producing results rather than
sitting in traffic. In addition, employee satisfaction is significantly higher.
There are environmental benefits from lower pollution levels, less traffic
congestion, and lower energy consumption, as well.

Job mobility

Structural shifts in the U.S. economy and the rising tide of permanent layoffs
have significantly increased job mobility. For example, between 1991 and
1996, median job-tenure levels for men ages 25–64 fell by an average of 19
percent. At the same time, there was unprecedented hiring and job creation
in many sectors. According to the Bureau of Labor Statistics, 2.6 million new
jobs were created in the United States in 1996.

Employees are becoming increasingly "portable." Most people will work for
four to five companies in their lifetimes. Individuals are more focused on
employment security than on job security. Those with highly transferable
skills continue to find employment, even if a specific job is eliminated at a
particular company.

Individual mobility

You never know who you will work with next. In the current, complex
environment, no one person can create and deliver all of the solutions that
clients require. Teams quickly form to solve problems—often with people who

have never before met—and dissolve just as rapidly as the participants move on to new issues and challenges. Team members may be known only by their voices and network identifications—some teams never work face-to-face. Increasingly, teams include individuals brought together from different disciplines, different companies, and different countries.

Growing numbers of workers are contract employees or employees who work for a firm as part of an outsourcing agreement. For the length of the contract they are indistinguishable from the "real" employees. When the contract ends, they move on to other firms. For some, this is a highly desirable employment pattern, affording individuals the opportunity to "shop around" for good employers and desirable positions.

Pace of Change

There is an accelerated rate of change in business and industry. Product cycles are now measured in months rather than years. For example, many computer products that used to be "refreshed" or redesigned every three years are now updated within six to nine months because the technology is changing so quickly.

There are substantial penalties for moving too slowly in business. One economic model shows that high-tech products that come to market six months late but on budget will earn one-third less profit over five years. In contrast, coming out on time and 50 percent over budget cuts profit by only 4 percent. The pace of change is reflected not just in the number of new products but also in the number of new companies that are emerging.

Change is difficult for individuals and organizations. The pace of change is one of the most significant challenges of the workplace. Staying ahead of the competition requires the ability to sense trends and evaluate what should stay the same and what should change. Once these analytical (or intuitive) decisions have been made, execution is required.

Productivity

The essence of management is to make knowledge productive (Drucker 1994). This not only implies that people do something with what they know, it also means that people share information that can lead to new knowledge or insight.

Maximizing creativity

How do companies reach the market with a more innovative product faster than the competition? How can they maximize responsiveness to customer needs? The creativity of employees and managers leads to new products, new

services, and more efficient operations.   The ability to see problems and
opportunities with "new eyes" confers a competitive advantage.

In the technology business, creativity might not be a descriptor immediately
mentioned by many.   Yet it is required in all phases of work.   Creativity is
required in management. How do you coax the best out of a disparate group of
individuals? Creativity is required in product development. Creativity is even
required to structure financing.   Although some individuals appear to be
inherently more "creative" than others, it is a mental process that can be
learned.

Getting results

The days of simply "putting in your time" are over for most employees.   The
key is creating value. Results count. Those who take action create value—for
themselves and for their organizations.   Strong encouragement is provided
when pay is tied to the performance of employees. Emphasis is placed on
incentives (e.g., bonuses) for meeting specific job goals.   In fact, standard
salary increases and predictable career advancement are becoming less certain
each year.

In business and industry the overwhelming experience is that "you get what
you reward."   Paying for results is logical in an environment where more and
more work is based around projects and less around a "job."   The transition has
not been easy, however.   Within many companies, the culture 10 years ago was
strongly oriented toward equating long hours with more work. A great deal of
manager and employee time was spent describing the job responsibilities.
Effort sometimes counted as much as effectiveness.   Today the approach is
oriented toward outcomes.   Many employees—from all levels—have had
difficulty adjusting to the notion that their superiors are not particularly
concerned with what they do on a daily basis or the number of hours they
work; they care about results.

As people have adjusted to the "pay-for-performance" transition, most are
highly supportive. Whether employees are paid for individual results, team
results, or the company's results, the emphasis is placed on measurable accomplishments.   A well-established trend in the United States, pay-for-performance, is now becoming more popular in Europe and Asia.

Security

For individual workers, brains, know-how, broad skills, and the willingness to
learn throughout life have become the essential tools for building careers in
which work with a single employer will be the exception, not the rule (ACE
1997). When asked, nearly two-thirds of adults say they have already changed
companies at least once since they started working.   One-third say they have
changed at least three times (Dillman et al. 1995).

Outsourcing

To enhance their flexibility to enter (or leave) segments of the market quickly, more and more companies are outsourcing selected functions. If a function is not part of the key skill set of the organization, it is a candidate for outsourcing. Bookkeeping, payroll, food service, janitorial services, and secretarial support are all common areas of outsourcing. This trend is expected to increase over time.

An increasing number of college graduates find themselves employed on contracts. Although most people have accepted that they will work for more than one firm in their lifetimes, coming to grips with a different employer every year is an order-of-magnitude different. The shifts in loyalty and frequent changes of corporate culture and operating procedures may be stimulating to some but unsettling to others.

However, outsourcing has strong appeal to a segment of the population. "Independents" may find this more attractive than traditional positions and career paths. For those "independents," maximizing flexibility and/or short-term income as a contractor is highly desirable.

Less job security

People expect career changes to become more common. The reasons stem from the accelerated rate of change in business and industry. Product cycles are rapid. A change in technology can spawn new industries almost overnight. The half-life of information is short, and knowledge doubles every few years. Businesses are revamping fundamental work processes and undergoing radical change. The job or career that existed yesterday may be gone tomorrow.

Because of rapid changes in business, outsourcing, and other trends, there will be less job security. Although many employers would like to provide better job security, it is often too expensive for many in a highly competitive, low-margin environment. If a company is downsizing, being a hard worker may not be enough to guarantee one's job. Ensuring that employees have skills that are valuable and transferable—from one company to another—is becoming increasingly important to both firms and individuals.

"In the new economy, don't expect to be taken care of by your large corporate employer, even if you go along with your company's program. Your job and security will depend on your own competence and work skills, not on the management hierarchy. That makes you responsible for staying on the cutting edge when it comes to skills development and knowledge of your business or profession and the market in which you compete. Assess your skills, find good teachers, and make time for self-improvement" (James 1996, 163).

Employment security in the 1990s and beyond will depend upon very different factors than in previous eras. No government, company, or union can realistically guarantee employment for life, increasing wages, or upward mobility. Within the new global marketplace an individual's economic security depends upon his or her own ability to adapt to the changing demands of jobs and of the job market. Employees who fare best in this environment are those with the skills, training, mobility, and flexibility to move laterally, as well as vertically, within organizations and the external labor market (Potter and Youngman 1997).

QUESTIONS TO ASK

- How well do our faculty, staff, and students understand the work environment? What kind of systemic changes should be made to enhance the faculty's understanding of the work environment? the staff's? the students'?
- What is our institution doing to help students prepare for the world of work?
- How well have changes in the curricula kept pace with the changes in the work environment?
- How often do we involve alumni who are working in business and industry in defining and evaluating your programs?
- What are our criteria for determining success in adapting programs to meet workplace needs?
- How well have institutional human resources policies, pay scales, and hiring practices adapted to professionals and technicians versus white-collar and blue-collar workers?
- Are career development and placement offices (or faculty advisors) helping students anticipate multiple career changes, outsourced positions, and reduced job security?
- Are career development and placement offices offering services to alumni who are shifting jobs or careers?

CHAPTER 2

Finding the Added Value

A highly educated population is seen as the key to economic growth and a stable society. Higher education's importance will continue to grow as the world's economic strength is increasingly based on an information age model. It has been estimated that 80 percent of the jobs in the United States within the next 20 years will be cerebral and only 20 percent manual—the exact opposite of the ratio in 1920 (James 1996). Although natural resources and manufacturing will always be necessary, wealth and power will be predicated on knowledge, creativity, and global communications. Can there be any question that higher education is important to business?

If you ask almost anyone in business or industry why they are concerned about higher education, three responses would dominate.

- We need employees who come to our businesses ready to work.
- We desperately need teachers who can help improve achievement in K–12 education.
- We need a system of lifelong learning for all of our citizens.

Without a strong education system, we cannot have strong communities; without strong communities, we cannot have strong businesses; and without these, we cannot have a strong economy or a strong democracy. Indeed, the fabric of our individual and collective aspirations is inextricably linked to a successful education system.

Education adds value to business and society through global competitiveness, the benefits that accrue to graduates (such as workforce preparation and their return on investment), quality of life, and continuous learning.

GLOBAL COMPETITIVENESS

Corporations, governments, and international organizations are calling for a more prominent role for education, from basic literacy to lifelong professional education. The rationale is the same worldwide: economic prosperity is linked to an educated workforce that can compete in a global economy where IT sets the pace of change.

For example, a policy document published in 1989 by the Confederation of British Industry calls for nothing short of a "skills revolution" — necessitating "urgent action" by Britain's education and training community — in order to maintain and improve Britain's competitive position in the world economy.

Heads of government attending the 1996 Group of Seven (G7) Summit, a meeting of the world's advanced industrial democracies, issued a communiqué pledging policy coordination to ensure that all citizens can benefit from the opportunities created by a new global economy. In doing so, the leaders reaffirmed their belief that investment in people is as vital as investment in capital, calling for improvements in basic education, lifelong skills formation, and training and school-to-work transitions. The most successful economies and societies will be those that focus on the long-term, by investing vigorously in training for their workers (G7 1996).

The Organization of Economic Cooperation and Development (OECD) has also recognized that the benefits of a global economy can be realized only if individuals, enterprises and countries show themselves capable of rapid adjustment and continuing innovation. One key to this is ensuring that everyone has a sound foundation for lifelong learning and can acquire the necessary qualifications and skills to enhance employability in an evolving labor market and knowledge-based society. The European Community, in advocating a European distance-learning service, predicts that, all things being equal, countries with higher levels of education and training will be the least affected by employment dislocation and other problems associated with global competitiveness. They believe that there can be no doubt that education and training, in addition to their fundamental task of promoting the development of the individual and the values of citizenship, have a key role to play in stimulating growth and restoring competitiveness and a socially acceptable level of employment in the community (ECISPO 1995).

The Esprit program, launched by the European Community in 1984, recently reorganized itself with a new mission focused on identifying and developing IT-based tools, processes, and applications that improve the competitiveness of organizations through supporting and enhancing the learning capability and effectiveness. The program seeks to promote innovation in such areas as collaborative learning and teamwork, virtual classrooms, computer-based simulation exercises, and decision-support systems.

Many developing nations have the capability to "leapfrog" the educational infrastructures and effectiveness of more developed countries. Their modest investment in any preexisting physical infrastructure and the potentially massive return on investment make the creation of national distance-learning networks an attractive proposition. "Given the trend toward more open societies and global economies, we must emphasize the forms of learning and critical thinking that enable individuals to understand changing environments, create new knowledge, and shape their own destinies. We must respond to new challenges by promoting learning in all aspects of life, through all institutions of society, in effect, creating environments in which living is learning" (UNESCO 1996).

BENEFITS OF A DEGREE

A study conducted in the United Kingdom identified a number of benefits of completing a college education. For many respondents in the study, the level of work and commitment that is involved in completing a degree was perceived to provide proof of being intellectually equipped for the world of work. Other benefits of a degree were categorized according to personal development, work preparation, and flexibility.

Personal Development

Many strategic and line managers see the undergraduate experience as having a major positive impact on the personal development of graduates. This personal development is considered at least as important as the intellectual benefits of a degree and often more important than the development of a specific knowledge base. College graduates believe that they are more mature, well-rounded people with a broader perspective on the world as a result of their undergraduate experience (Harvey et al. 1997).

Work Preparation

Although students find selected elements of their degree programs relevant, much is perceived to have little value. The development of broad skills, such as the ability to communicate, are seen as the most meaningful (Harvey et al. 1997).

In a recent ACE study, corporate leaders explained that today's college graduates are impressive—in most cases as good as or better than their predecessors—but that they are not well qualified to lead in the workplace given today's dramatically changing conditions. The problem is not that today's graduates are less skilled than those of previous generations, but that expectations for performance are much higher today than ever before.

Business leaders highlighted several areas in which they believe recent graduates are deficient:

- communication skills
- the ability to work in teams
- flexibility
- the ability to accept ambiguity comfortably
- the ability to work with people from diverse backgrounds
- understanding of globalization and its implications
- adequate ethics training

This study parallels what others have found, i.e., that although many graduates considered that their degrees were enormously beneficial both in personal and work-related terms, a large number considered that the undergraduate experience did not adequately prepare them for the world of work. Nine out of 10 suggested that the degree equipped them for *getting* a job rather than performing in the workplace.

According to one employer, "When you take a graduate on, they are very good conceptually. The negative side of that is that they can be too thorough and it can take far too long. They know everything there is to know about design but when it comes to practicalities like printing it, they are on another planet. So you take a graduate who is a good designer and then you have to teach them about processing that design. For example, if somebody wants a brochure designed they will come up with a brilliant concept, but by the time they have finished with their design the client can't afford it, it's gone way over budget, there is no practical way it can be used, and they will think in three to six months' schedule whereas we think in three to six days" (Harvey et al. 1997, 86).

Employees also stressed the need for a more serious and comprehensive introduction to the demands of the work world. They suggested more sustained attention to the "nuts and bolts" of corporate life, including an introduction to its politics and norms and an overview of the personal behaviors expected in it. In addition, they called for more work opportunities; and suggested the use of more case studies and team-building activities (ACE 1997).

There was a feeling that direct practical application of techniques was missing from most undergraduate experiences, with the exception of those who had internships. Advice on how to present and sell oneself in the employment situation was also lacking. For some, the undergraduate course created unreal expectations of the world of work.

Many respondents thought their undergraduate courses lacked any real meaningful engagement with the world of work. One graduate considered that this lack of engagement was due to academic staff having no current involvement in industry.

> My experience of higher education institutions is that a lot of the lecturing staff that are in the establishments haven't got the experience of working in outside industry, and I think that is a significant drawback, for the simple reason that they don't understand what is actually needed out there in the working environment. It helps to have been in an office, or to have been outside to see what is going on rather than reading journals. They tend to get too involved in the theoretical side of things rather than becoming practically involved, and I don't think the current lecturing staff that there is in higher education is going to be actually flexible enough to meet the demands of people in the future or provide them with the necessary level of understanding to actually get on in a modern working environment.

> Most found that the expectations in the work situation were tantamount to a culture shock. "Although I have worked for people before during vacations, suddenly being thrust into the work place I didn't know what to expect…Here they tend to throw you in with a customer and you get on with it. I don't suppose when you leave university you really know how to deal with other people let alone a customer where you have to behave in a certain manner. (Harvey et al. 1997, 85–86)

Flexibility

In comparisons of higher education graduates versus those without college or university degrees, graduates were seen as more adaptable and flexible and able to develop new ideas. "I think that the skill in graduates is the ability to be flexible, to have a broad knowledge base with a number of different subjects, but to have a level of intellectual ability, and I think that particularly in terms of problem solving, through doing a degree and going through that discipline" (Harvey et al. 1997, 89). Graduates were also seen as more mature, with broader outlooks, as more self-motivated, committed, tenacious, enthusiastic, energized, or ambitious.

Graduates generally thought they had more to offer, including being more academic, stretchable, versatile, ambitious, flexible, and well rounded; being quicker to grasp things; having a wider view; and being more suitable as "management material."

Most managers thought graduates were basically brighter, sharper, and more analytical than non-graduates. "The advantage of a graduate over a non-graduate is probably they are more self-assured and usually they have a much better idea of how to think things through. So posed with a problem, most of them usually approach it working it through from a to b, whereas a non-graduate will usually go on experience of what happened in the past and solve it that way" (Harvey et al. 1997, 88).

RETURN ON INVESTMENT

For a large proportion of its clientele, education is an investment—a down payment on a career, social status, or more immediately, a job. Most students take the degrees they do to get the jobs they want, knowing or hoping that these jobs will repay the investment (Brown and Duguid 1996). A high school graduate earns 37 percent more than a high school dropout. A person with one to three years of college (including associate's or vocational degrees) earns 18 percent more than a high school graduate. A college graduate with a B.A. degree or higher earns 47 percent more than a person with one to three years of college (NAB 1997e).

Today's increased demand for higher education emerges from economic aspirations and from the certain knowledge that a college degree now provides a greater marginal increase in economic security than it ever has. This demand is from new kinds of students, often of an age with which the system is still relatively unfamiliar, and often from family circumstances and patterns of work commitment vastly different from our past experience (Kennedy 1995).

It is not just the demand for two-year or four-year degrees that has grown. The need for advanced education is also increasing. A greater percentage of the world's population needs to be educated to be productive in an increasingly technological workplace. Particular skills are relevant for a shorter period, so the need for lifelong learning is growing. Plus, the knowledge and skills necessary to function at the frontier of knowledge are expanding, increasing the need for advanced degrees (Wulf 1995).

Education has broad economic returns that go beyond the individual. For every dollar Illinois invests in undergraduates at the University of Illinois, taxes return $4.31 to the state over time. This study concluded that a college education yields a 6 percent real (inflation-adjusted) return on the investment. A male college graduate would earn $1,028,463 more than a high school graduate by age 74. The conclusion about the value of higher education is that students get a reasonably priced college education and the state gets more taxes on the higher income (Kangas 1997). A similar study involving the University of Iowa found that state funds generated roughly 10 times the economic activity of what is invested in education (Backhaus and Whiteman 1994). Another study using the University of Massachusetts at Boston (UMass/ Boston) concluded that UMass/Boston has been an extraordinarily lucrative investment for Massachusetts. The University of Massachusetts at Boston is a net revenue producer for the state government because of the projected future income of its students and because of the "export base" income it generates (i.e., spending of students with local businesses). The bottom line is that UMass/Boston returns each year to state coffers substantially more in personal and sales tax revenue than it receives in state support (Bluestone 1993).

College and universities stimulate economic growth through the creation of new jobs, as well. Using the Massachusetts Institute of Technology (MIT) as an example, a study found that the 4,000 companies founded by MIT graduates or faculty (as of 1994) employed 1.1 million people and generated $232 billion in world sales. In the United States, MIT-related companies employed 733,000 people or one out of every 170 jobs in the country (Kindleberger 1997).

QUALITY OF LIFE

Higher education is about more than productivity in the workplace. Enabling students to live productive lives in a knowledge-based economy will not be enough if we pay too little attention to enabling them to live meaningful lives. Quality of life is linked, in many ways, to higher education. It is no accident that many of the most vibrant centers for business have strong higher education institutions in the area (e.g., Silicon Valley, Calif., Research Triangle Park, N.C.). The quality of life in these areas attracts more business, in turn.

Irrespective of age, students will be challenged to contend with the moral ambiguities of a rapidly changing, chaotic world. Education helps provide students with the spiritual and psychological foundations to find their places in an uncertain world. The turbulence of contemporary change may be best understood and dealt with against the background of history, literature, and other disciplines that connect us with the broader human experience. In addition, the ability of a democratic populous to make informed decisions—the Jeffersonian ideal of an educated democracy—requires a broad education (Hooker 1997).

There is more to education than subject-matter expertise. Although Americans work more hours than in other western societies, there is a portion of time allocated to leisure. The arts, humanities, and sports have a role in education. (It is not necessarily an academic role for everyone, however.) Colleges and universities are uniquely capable of developing a well-rounded person.

CONTINUOUS LEARNING

The percentage of the U.S. population seeking postsecondary education has grown steadily during the twentieth century. This demand is likely to increase. Although a portion of escalating enrollments will be motivated by the belief that a college education is a starting point for a good career, the largest growth will come from (1) an adult population seeking to stay up-to-date in their chosen field, (2) those changing careers, and (3) "recreational" learners seeking new knowledge for the sake of that knowledge.

Business leaders agree that a broad education emphasizing flexible skills is essential in today's rapidly changing world because learning does not end when students receive their diplomas; rather, education is a continuous process (ACE 1997). The career stability of our parents is gone. Today, estimates are that current workers will move through from three to five careers. The predicted number of careers for those now graduating from college is closer to 13. With these kinds of career shifts, getting educated once is not enough. Some suggest that many information age workers will need to spend at least 20 percent of their time engaged in learning. Another estimate suggests that individuals in the workforce in 2000 may need to accumulate the equivalent of 30 credit hours of instruction every seven years. If this comes to pass, it will generate more than 20 million full-time-equivalent (FTE) learners from the workforce alone. Using our existing educational model, these learners would require hundreds of additional campuses enrolling perhaps 30,000 students apiece. To meet the potential demand by 2010, a new campus would have to be opened every eight days (Dolence and Norris 1995).

This is not an issue just for American higher education. Dolence and Norris (1995) extrapolate the number of FTE learners from the workforce in the United States and nine other industrialized countries. Even at a lower rate of retraining, the potential learning pool is more than 100 million FTE learners and 3,300 campuses. This does not even begin to address the increasing demand for higher education in developing countries.

Society has entered an era of "upskilling" where an individual continuously enhances his or her skills and competencies. Employees are increasingly empowered with the responsibility for their own ongoing education. Among the skills they will likely need to hone or acquire are problem solving, information processing, decision making, communications, and interpersonal skills. In addition to all of these, in the new global organization "international" skills or the ability to deal with global problems, opportunities, languages, and cultural differences will be much more critical.

A model of one-time education has decreasing relevance in a world and workplace defined by rapid change. Skill and education requirements are constantly changing to address new opportunities as well as new demands created by the introduction of new technology. One study found that more than half of the employees with bachelor's degrees have been encouraged by their employers to get more job-related education or training. However, the way people acquire knowledge changes as they get older. People ages 18–20 are most likely to have taken a course for college credit in the last three years, while those ages 40–45 and 50–64 are most likely to have taken a short course, seminar, or workshop (Dillman et al. 1995).

Most Americans accept that lifelong learning has become a reality. Seeking additional education and training throughout one's adult life is now the norm. Among those who are not retired:

- a large majority of adults—81 percent—think that getting additional training or education is important for them to be successful in their work
- a similarly large majority—80 percent—have received some kind of job-related training or education in the last three years
- almost three-fourths say they are interested in getting college education or training in the future
- over half say they will definitely or probably take a college course for credit in the next three years—75 percent say they'll take a non-credit college course (Dillman et al. 1995)

CONCLUSION

Higher education is of critical importance to business. It provides us with educated employees, educated consumers who purchase the products and services business produces, and an educated citizenry. More than ever before, the quality and accessibility of education will be the competitive differentiator of businesses and nations. The potential value added to society by education is already immense, but it has the opportunity to grow.

QUESTIONS TO ASK

- Are faculty and students aware of the growing global concern for education and its importance to economic development?
- What is our institution doing to ensure that students, faculty, and staff develop a foundation in lifelong learning skills?
- Do we know what skills and experiences our graduates consider most valuable as preparation for their careers?
- In what ways can our institution improve student preparation for performing in the workplace, not just getting their first jobs?
- In what ways could we improve students' realistic expectations of the world of work?
- In what ways could higher education add more value to students' educational experiences?
- In what ways can higher education add more value to graduates' lifelong educational experiences?
- How will our higher education institutions cope with the demand expected from 100 million FTE learners?
- Are students aware of the global context surrounding their own areas of study?

PART TWO

• • • • • • • • • • • •

Changes to Come

CHAPTER 3

Profiling the Customer

How competent and competitive we are—as businesses, institutions, and individuals—depends to a great extent on who we are and how we relate to society's needs. Business is being reshaped by demographics. Marketers are already cultivating generation Y, youngsters who have a projected $100 billion-plus annual buying power. The "baby boom" generation is beginning to focus on retirement. The fact that there will be more women and minorities in the workplace as well as in colleges and universities carries implications for what we do and how we do it. People will be working longer and changing careers more often. They will need training, education, and retraining. Understanding who we are and our needs is an important step in determining what business will need from higher education.

TODAY'S STUDENTS

The Distribution of Learners

If we were to do an analysis of the higher education market, we would find six distinct groups of learners.

- **Group 1:** 3.9 million traditional undergraduate students—ages 17–24, seeking bachelor's degrees, and enrolled full time at campuses
- **Group 2:** 650,000 traditional graduate students—ages 22–34, seeking either academic or professional master's or doctoral degrees and enrolled full time at campuses

- **Group 3:** 2.9 million semi-traditional undergraduate students—ages 17–24, seeking bachelor's degrees and enrolled part time at campuses, usually working part time in non-career, entry-level jobs
- **Group 4:** 487,000 semi-traditional graduate students—ages 22–34, seeking academic master's or doctoral degrees and enrolled part time at campuses (Employment varies among this population; some have part-time work in a variety of campus and off-campus non-career jobs. Others work in full-time careers, e.g., schoolteachers, principals, and superintendents or college teachers completing doctoral degrees.)
- **Group 5:** 5.3 million non-traditional undergraduate students—ages 25 and up, who are career-oriented members of the labor force, usually seeking first degrees in on-campus or off-campus programs, enrolled full or part time
- **Group 6:** 880,000 non-traditional graduate students—ages 25 and up, working full time in chosen careers, enrolled full or part time, seeking professional master's or doctoral degrees in on-campus or off-campus programs (Sperling and Tucker 1997)

The population of learners is older, more diverse, and more time-constrained than ever before. How well do our existing structures and service delivery systems work for these learners?

Students in groups 1– 4 are those typically thought of as the consumers of higher education, although they make up only 56 percent of the higher education student population. The remaining 44 percent (groups 5 and 6) are adults, mostly working, whose numbers are growing and who, by the twenty-first century, will make up half the higher education student population. Groups 1– 4 are served by traditional colleges and universities, i.e., institutions with tenured, full-time faculties; comprehensively equipped main campuses; and, often, residential facilities for students. Those institutions provide the desired educational services and have adequate capacity to meet the needs of traditional students for the future. They do not provide the educational systems and services needed and wanted by working adult students, nor do they have the capacity to satisfy this growing segment of the student population (Sperling and Tucker 1997).

The democratization of higher education is one of postwar America's greatest accomplishments. Half the workforce now passes through college. Yet American higher education cannot rest on its laurels.

Unfortunately, a large number of students leave higher education without any token of achievement, for example:

- first-year failure rates are 60–70 percent
- the first year is often extended to 18 months due to closed sections of basic, introductory courses in English and mathematics

- a 28 percent loss rate occurs between the first and second years
- satisfactory completion rates for the basic courses (e.g., English, math, chemistry) are 64 percent
- in community colleges only 9 percent of the students who come wanting associate degrees actually secure them
- at four-year institutions, less than 40 percent of the students receive bachelor's degrees within seven years
- graduation rates for all but the most selective institutions are in the 43–53 percent range (Twigg 1997)

Beyond the increasing numbers of non-traditional students and the challenges represented by these completion rates, more changes are coming.

More students entering the pipeline

School enrollment is projected to grow more than 8 percent between 1996 and 2001. The largest projected growth is in high school graduates. Their numbers are expected to increase by about 19 percent nationally (Marks 1996). After five years of relative stability in higher education enrollments, U.S. colleges and universities now seem poised on the edge of extremely rapid growth. Based on the demographics alone, an increase of some 2 million college students is expected in the next 10 years.

Add to this the increase in older and employed students seeking skills enhancement and other forms of continuing education (or retraining), and the numbers go much higher. In total, the demand for higher education is greater than most of our states and local governments can handle under the existing model.

More students will attend part time

Nearly half of the college and university students pursuing degrees now attend on a part-time basis—6.6 million in 1993, up from fewer than 3 million in 1970. The number of full-time students grew just 38 percent over the same period. Older part-time students, particularly women, kept higher education enrollment stable even while the traditional college-age population suffered a temporary decline because of the baby-bust generation (Speer 1996).

More students will attend public institutions

Public institutions now enroll nearly 80 percent of the nation's college students, or 11.1 million of the 14.3 million students. It is tempting to speculate that this trend is due to college costs. For students at public institutions, tuition averages around $2,000 per year. The 2.9 million students who attend private four-year colleges pay approximately $12,000 in tuition and fees. Even without distinctions of public versus private, enrollments are highly concentrated. Four hundred ten campuses accounted for more than 50 percent of the total enrollment in U.S. higher education (Green 1997). Out of a possible

3,600 institutions of higher education, this represents a significant concentration of students.

More students will attend two-year institutions

The two-year college enrollment growth rate from the late 1980s to the early 1990s (more than 20 percent) was double the growth rate in four-year colleges (approximately 11 percent). Nearly half of the total enrollment growth from the early 1980s to the early 1990s occurred in two-year colleges. The number of associate degrees earned from the mid-1980s to the early 1990s rose more than 15 percent (Marks 1996).

More students will attend proprietary institutions

Enrollment in postsecondary education will continue to increase. However, the share of students in different types of institutions will change. More students are enrolling in for-profit institutions where programs range from truck driving to network management. Many of these certificate programs are not offered in traditional postsecondary institutions.

Share of Postsecondary Education Market by Year Percentage Change in Enrollment			
	1986–94	1996	2010
4-year institutions	12	57	49
2-year institutions	18	34	35
Proprietary institutions	42	9	16

Source: National Association of Business (NAB). 1997d. Paper from Business Policy Council for Workforce Development, 21 May.

Enrollments are concentrated

Large undergraduate enrollments are concentrated in relatively few academic areas. Forty-four to 52 percent of community college enrollment is concentrated in 25 courses; 35 percent of baccalaureate enrollment is in these same courses. Put another way, about 1 percent of the nation's courses generates nearly half of its total enrollment. The "1 percent" course titles include introductory studies in English, mathematics, psychology, sociology, economics, accounting, biology, and chemistry. In many large institutions, those courses are not "owned" by individual faculty members in the same way as are advanced level courses. They are frequently not "owned" by any curriculum in particular but serve as feeders to multiple programs (Twigg 1997).

Students are older

Although the 18–24-year-old population is still the largest group on college campuses, enrollments are increasing among students 25 years and older.

More than half of all undergraduates are 22 years or older and almost a quarter are 30 years or older.

> ...the real story in the [higher education] enrollment upturn has been the dramatic increase in the number of adults on college campuses over the past two decades. Although most images of 'college life' still focus on younger students enrolled in residential institutions, the college market is clearly no longer a 'youth' market. From 1970 to 1991, adult enrollments almost tripled, jumping from 2.3 to 6.5 million. Currently, more than 40% of the 'students' enrolled in two- or four-year colleges and universities in the United States are age 25 or older. By 1998, the age 25 and over enrollment will account for 5 of every 11 students attending U.S. colleges and universities—some 7 million students out of a projected enrollment of 15.1 million. Moreover, enrollment projections from the National Center for Education Statistics (NCES 1995) indicate that by 1998 the number of 'students' on college campuses who are 35 and over will surpass those in the 18- to 19-year old population—the group that most campuses (and college marketers) have traditionally viewed as the core clientele in higher education. (Green 1996, 24)

Students are more likely to be female and/or minorities

Women now outnumber men in undergraduate and graduate schools and approach 40 percent of the students enrolled in professional programs (Marks 1996). Between 1984 and 1994, the total enrollment in higher education increased by about 2 million, or 16 percent. Not one of the students contributing to this rise was a European-American male. Seventy-one percent were students classified as African American, Native American, Asian American, and Latin American. The remaining 29 percent were nonresident aliens (up 36 percent) and European-American women. People classified as "minority" or "foreign" now account for 28.8 percent of all students in higher education (Menand 1997).

The types of degrees and areas of specialization are changing

Certificates are a growing part of the education market. Bachelor of Arts (B.A.) degrees represent 60 percent of all awards, while Associate of Arts (A.A.) degrees represent 28 percent of the market.

| | Growth in Certificates | |
Degrees Conferred	1984–85 % of total	1993–94 % of total
Awards/Certificates	8	12
Associate's Degrees	28	28
Bachelor's Degrees	64	60

Source: National Association of Business (NAB). 1997d. Paper from Business Policy Council for Workforce Development, 21 May.

In addition, the mix of disciplines for both degrees and awards/certificates is changing.

| **Shifts in Fields of Study** | | | |
| **Percentage Change from 1984–85 to 1993–94** | | | |
Field of Study	Awards/Certificates	Associate's Degrees	Bachelor's Degrees
Computer Science	87	-25	-38
Engineering Technologies	-18	-25	-16
Precision Production	21	11	-24
Education	86	32	22
Business Administration	-14	-15	6
General/Liberal Studies	138	55	53

Source: National Association of Business (NAB). 1997e. The multifaceted returns to education. <http://www.nab.com/econ/returntoed.html>.

Financial Concerns for Learners

Student tuition and fees continue to rise

Inflation has tripled consumer prices since 1973–74. At public two-year colleges, tuition and fees have quadrupled, and at public universities they have increased almost five times. Tuition and fees at private universities have risen the most—they now stand at six times their 1973–74 level (Marks 1996).

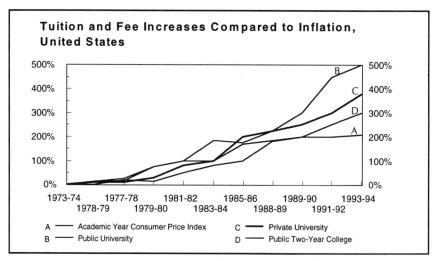

Source: Marks, Joseph L. 1996. *SREB Fact Book on Higher Education* (1994/1995). Atlanta: Southern Regional Education Board, 91. Data from National Center for Education Statistics, U.S. Bureau of Labor Statistics.

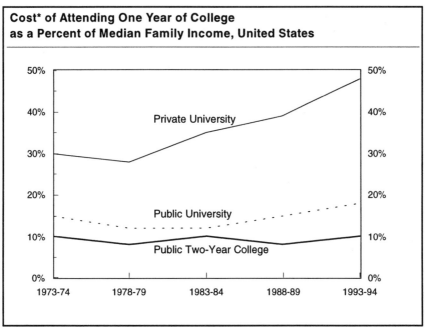

Cost* of Attending One Year of College as a Percent of Median Family Income, United States

*Cost consists of undergraduate in-state tuition, required fees, room, and board.
Source: Marks, Joseph L. 1996. *SREB Fact Book on Higher Education* (1994/1995). Atlanta: Southern Regional Education Board, 92. Data from National Center for Education Statistics, U.S. Bureau of Labor Statistics.

Nationally, the annual cost of attending one year at a private university has risen from 29 percent of median family income to almost 48 percent on average over the past 20 years. During the same period, the cost of attending one year at a public university rose from 13 percent to 16 percent of the median family income, while public two-year college annual costs remained between 9 percent and 10 percent. When adjusted for inflation, median family income rose almost 10 percent, public university costs rose 34 percent, public two-year college costs rose 3 percent, and private university costs rose 88 percent (Marks 1996).

Impact on lower income students

The echo of the baby boom will produce an increase of about one-third the size of the traditional college-age population over the next decade. With growing demand for places and limited fiscal resources, it seems likely that state institutions will respond by raising tuition and by continuing to restrict admission at the more prestigious public campuses to students with better academic preparation and therefore, on average, more affluent backgrounds. This trend seems likely to exacerbate the stratification of public higher education by income (McPherson and Schapiro 1996).

Tuition rates will have an impact, as well. Increases in net cost over time lead to decreases in enrollment rates for lower income students. For lower income students a $150 net cost increase, expressed in 1993–94 dollars, results in a 1.6 percent decline in enrollment for that income group (McPherson and Schapiro 1996).

If appropriate steps are not taken, higher education could become so expensive that millions of students will be denied access. Average real tuition per student, adjusted for inflation, approximately doubled in the 20 years from 1976 to 1995. If tuition doubles again in the next 20-year period (1996–2015), about 6.7 million students will be priced out of the system. In other words, about one out of every two people we would expect to seek a college education will not be able to pay for it. Even if tuition increases by only 25 percent over the 20 years, one out of five students will be excluded (CAE 1997).

GENERATIONAL DIFFERENCES

The last decade has seen a significant increase in products, services, and marketing that targets different age groups. Construction of retirement homes in warm climates, financial services, and health care are only the beginning of the list of tailored services for our aging population. Age and expectations can have a significant impact on what learners want and need from education. The biggest changes are likely to come from opposite ends of the age spectrum.

Generation Y

Marketers have coined the term "generation Y" for those children who will hit their teen years just as the next century dawns. The teenage population will reach 30 million by 2006, the highest level since 1975. We are already seeing the impact—elementary and middle schools seem to be bursting at the seams.

Attention is being paid to this generation because of their immense buying power. The group has a projected $100 billion-plus annual purchasing power. Schools are already a hot marketing venue (Graham 1997). Along with goods, this generation will consume education at a phenomenal rate. Yet generation Y will be hitting colleges and universities at a time when government support for higher education is more austere. It may be that spending on higher education will be pitted against spending on Medicare. No one knows which generation will "win."

Irrespective of the economics, generation Y will be the first generation of learners to take the Internet for granted; they will never know a world without computers. Generation Y's orientation in space and time will be different from its predecessors'. Some are growing up with online pen pals in Europe or Asia. Global conversations—even chess games—over the Internet will bring distant cultures close. Far more than today, their world will be global, connected, and around-the-clock (Graham 1997). What's more, they won't even realize how remarkable that is. This generation views computers as basic equipment, like pencil and paper, not something to be feared (Beck 1997).

Technologically, this generation is going to make the generation Xers look like fuddy-duddies. Nearly 60 percent of households with children ages seven or younger have personal computers. Predictions are that within five years, members of generation Y will be producing term papers with full-motion video. They are on fast-forward (Beck 1997).

However, not all of generation Y is growing up on computers. By the time generation Y enters college, the have and have-not dilemma may have reached serious proportions.

Aging Population

The aging of our population is likely to produce a variety of changes in society at large as well as in higher education. In a world oriented toward the lifestyles of the elderly, almost every aspect of society will undergo dramatic revision, ranging from health to security to entertainment. Other shifts may result from the fact that the next generation of seniors will be far more energetic and better educated than its predecessors. The increasing presence of senior citizens may represent a windfall of sorts for colleges and universities that are alert to the possibilities. The opportunities that campuses present for "continued learning" already are acknowledged by programs such as Elderhostel (Trachtenberg 1997).

It will continue to be important for business and higher education to think about the implications of our changing population. Trachtenberg (1997) predicts that professors at institutions that decide to encourage enrollment by senior citizens will face a remarkable intellectual challenge in dealing with the "already taught." The baby boomers, as senior citizens and returning students, would confront their instructors with a new kind of adult student. Unlike many students of recent decades, the aging baby boomers would not be taking courses to improve their credentials or their careers; intellectual curiosity is likely to be the underlying motive for a return to the classroom. Their teachers may well feel that they are confronting classes of eager assistants, rather than relatively passive learners. Senior citizen baby boomers will bring to bear on class discussion whole lifetimes of experience. For the instructor, the experience could be both exhilarating and exhausting.

THE CHANGING PROFESSORIATE

Decline of Full-time Tenured and Tenure-track Professors

The traditional concept of the professoriate is being supplemented by new hiring and promotion arrangements across the United States, and in other countries as well. The proportion of faculty in tenured and tenure-track positions is steadily declining in many countries. In the United States, approximately 35 percent of all faculty are part timers, and more than one-third of the full-time faculty hold term appointments (Altbach and Maassen 1997).

The full-time tenured and tenure-track professoriate will very likely continue to decline as a proportion of the academic workforce, although it will remain the "gold standard" to which all aspire. The traditional faculty are those who perform the complex governance functions of the institution. They serve on committees, design new curricula, become department chairs, fill the senior administrative positions of the university, and produce most of the research. Indeed, the statutes of most colleges and universities reserve full participation in governance, including voting on important academic decisions, to the full-time, tenured, or tenure-track faculty.

Increase in Part-time Faculty

The traditional faculty ranks may constitute half (or even less) of the profession. The new and growing middle category of full-time but non-tenure-track faculty is growing rapidly. Hired mainly to teach, individuals in these new ranks teach more, are not expected to engage in research, and have only a limited role in institutional governance. They receive the standard benefits from the institution, but their terms of appointment are limited by contract to five years or some other finite period. Paid somewhat less than tenure-track faculty, these staff members are part of the academic community but not fully involved in the affairs of the university.

Part-time faculty have been part of the academic landscape for a long time, and they are a rapidly growing part of the academic labor force. They are hired to teach a specific course or two, provided no benefits, often given no office space, and expected simply to show up to teach a class. They are paid very modestly on a per-course basis. Not surprisingly, part-time faculty feel little loyalty to the institution (Altbach and Maassen 1997).

Professorial Perception

While there is a perception that things are modestly deteriorating in academe, there is certainly no groundswell from the professoriate for greater emphasis on teaching, new procedures for assessment, or a reorientation of American higher education (Altbach and Maassen 1997).

The full-time American academic profession remains largely insulated from the broad changes taking place in higher education. According to a recent survey, they seem to have little understanding of these trends, do not see them as a crisis, and do not recognize them as part of a permanent change in the landscape of American higher education. They have not yet experienced the new realities for themselves—part-time status, contract employment, etc. Presidents and other leaders have not communicated the idea that faculty have a responsibility for institutional adjustment and survival nor have they involved the professoriate in responding to financial and other realities (Altbach and Maassen 1997).

The Carnegie survey, conducted by Altbach and Maassen (1997), reveals an academic profession that has a vague sense of unease but little sense of crisis. The difficulties of academe are evident elsewhere. Britain has seen the most far-reaching reform, with the abolition of the tenure system, the amalgamation of the polytechnics with the universities to more than double the size of the university system, the imposition of performance measures for teaching and research, and the allocation of funds to universities based on these measures.

In China and other countries, universities are increasingly asked to generate their own revenues. Chinese universities, in addition to charging tuition and fees to students, have also established consulting departments, profit-making laboratories, and even businesses in many fields. Peking University, China's most prestigious academic institution, runs a successful software company and other enterprises (Altbach and Maassen 1997).

CONCLUSION

The professoriate is changing. The composition of today's students and the significant shifts likely in the next decade all point to change. Business and higher education will be faced with more individuals who come from increasingly diverse backgrounds and disparate academic preparation. To even the casual observer, business as usual is not likely to be adequate.

Business and higher education are being reshaped by demographics. It will be up to us and our institutions whether we see our changing population as an opportunity.

QUESTIONS TO ASK

- Do we know the age, gender, and ethnic breakdown of our students? Do we know what attracts them to our institution?
- How are our current students affected by the growing number of part-time students? Of older students?

- Should we make changes to our educational programs or delivery options to accommodate different types of learners? Do they represent a new category of customers?
- What are our competitors doing about these trends?
- What does the institution stand to gain if we adapt to these learners? What do we stand to lose?
- Can our society and economy afford to lose one-fifth to one-half of the potential student population because higher education has become too costly?

CHAPTER 4

Information Technology as a Change Agent

nformation technology is changing how we work and live. It is changing our behavior—as individuals and as institutions. Most of us have come to rely on e-mail and voice mail. Personalized greeting cards and "virtual flowers" are sent via the Internet by millions. The excitement generated by vicariously exploring the surface of Mars in near real-time may produce a new generation of astronomers and geologists. In short, technology is a powerful force for change. Some contend that it is as powerful as the electric light, the printing press, manned flight or any of the other technologies that have fundamentally altered the world. Information technology is a fundamental change agent that will result in individual, social, and organizational shifts.

One reason that IT acts as a change agent is that the speed and magnitude of the alterations it catalyzes are so dramatic. Consider the automobile as an example of the transformative effects of technology. In 1985 the most expensive car made in the United States was a Cadillac. It cost $17,000, averaged 12 miles to the gallon, and weighed more than 1 ton. If the automobile industry had achieved the same technology trajectory as the computer industry, today a Cadillac would cost $12.63, weigh 14 pounds, get 5,900 miles to the gallon, and be 3 feet long! In fact, if you are driving a Ford Taurus today, you are "piloting" a vehicle that contains more computing power than the first lunar landing module.

In addition to technological changes, there are often significant unforeseen consequences of a given technology. The introduction of the automobile changed this country irreversibly within a few decades. It changed where we work, changed the way we live, moved us from the cities to the suburbs, and created the shopping mall. Who was the great visionary who foresaw all of these changes? Who were the planners who guided us through the transition? The truth is it just happened. It overpowered us with the relentless force of a new paradigm. If we had planned—even a little bit—we probably would not have chosen some of the outcomes.

"Consider computing and communications technologies. Already they have changed the way we work and created the major industry of our times. For some, it has already changed the way they court and the way they work. There is preliminary evidence of changes in living patterns due to telecommuting. We can engage the process or we can just let it happen. In either case, happen it will" (Wilson 1997, 111). Technology is inexorable.

CHANGES IN TECHNOLOGY

Technically, there are four major trends that are behind many of these changes: digitization, storage, the increase in processing power, and universal communications. All four have an impact on business and higher education.

Digitization

Information technology makes it possible to digitize information. Whether text, images, sound, or large data streams, digitization has allowed us to effectively create a worldwide "language" with which to communicate. Virtually everything can be translated into a common currency of bits and bytes.

Powerful new communications technologies are giving networks the bandwidth needed to handle rich but space-consuming digitized information such as video, medical images, and great works of art. Networks are developing the speed to support interaction, enabling two-way communication and collaboration. Digital content carried over high-speed networks makes the once improbable entirely possible.

Storage

Add to this trend another. The capacity of data storage devices is growing by 60 percent each year, and data access rates are increasing dramatically. The result is that digital storage of information is increasingly efficient and convenient. Digital magnetic storage is already less costly than paper and will continue to be the dominant medium for the storage of active data. Even denser storage—densities of 3 billion bits per square inch have been recorded—which allows the text of 375 average-sized novels to be stored in a single square inch of disk surface. CD-ROMs are rapidly becoming the preferred storage and publishing medium for text, images, full-motion video, electronic catalogs, games, and software. Current prototypes of multilayer optical disks (with 10 disks)—a high-density CD—have the capability to store 6 billion bytes of information, equivalent to more than 1 million pages of text.

The result is that we can now store and integrate all kinds of information to create more powerful and engaging educational, entertainment, or informational material.

Processing Power

The processing power at our disposal has increased tremendously over time. In the first half of the twentieth century, eletromechanical machines punched, tabulated, and sorted cards at high speed. Wires, wheels, and levers formed our early processors. Soon, even the fastest punch card machines were bypassed by technological change—the vacuum tube. The electronic computer incorporated vacuum tubes as well as a "stored program" concept that expanded the machine's ability to do complex work at high speed. Transistors gave birth to the next generation of computer technology. Replacing vacuum tubes with transistors shortened the time needed for electrical pulses to complete a circuit. It all sounds archaic when compared to the silicon chips that now dominate the computer industry.

The rapid growth in microprocessor performance will continue; expect performance to double every 18 months. Clock rates will continue to move ahead rapidly, exceeding 1 GHz or billions of instructions per second by the next decade. By 2000, a typical client microprocessor will have the capability of today's large servers.

Universal Communications

In this decade, we will move beyond client-server computing and packet-based Internet connections to global connectivity, which will profoundly change access to content, services, and communications.

Wireless communications and increasing bandwidth will change the landscape, enabling transparent access across all networks. Things will work together without being wired together—transceivers will be built into most products. Personal area networks (PANs) will be pervasive. Local area networks (LANs) will be ubiquitous, with integrated voice and data. Radio frequency will be used within individual buildings or small campuses, and infrared will be used within rooms or other enclosed spaces. Wide area networks (WANs) will provide worldwide universal access through technologies such as cellular digital packet data, satellite networks, and two-way paging. Communication-device form factors, i.e., the size of the "computer," will decrease while function increases, resulting in wearable computers. Imagine a wristwatch that can receive messages and send acknowledgments!

As function, portability, and battery life improve, our digital tool kit will always be with us. Automatic intermittent wireless connections will ensure that we have instant access to anything we need, wherever we are. Software sophistication, user interfaces and systems management will continue to improve. As a result, users will become increasingly comfortable interacting with computer systems. More and more, individuals will get connected and stay connected.

There are likely to be several results from these technological changes. First, everyone will become a technology user because costs will be low enough and compatibility will be high. New software will allow the broader population of users to easily deal with ever more complex systems. Second, integration within and among organizations will become pervasive. We already see this in the form of electronic links among suppliers, distributors, and customers. Finally, we will process and transport bits instead of things and people. In many cases information will displace the physical. Working this way will be faster and less costly, as well as less harmful to the environment. The result is that we will be living in a networked world.

THE NETWORKED WORLD

Largely due to improvements in digitization, processing power, storage, and communications, we have created a networking revolution. Higher education will have a crucial role in developing these capabilities as well as training and educating those who will use them.

This global network is expected to add billions of dollars to the world economy. Advances in storing and compressing digitized data, combined with advances in distribution systems and proliferation of low earth orbiting satellite (LEOS) networks are bringing education, entertainment, and services to even the most remote parts of the globe. New job opportunities will be created in the processing, organizing, packaging, and dissemination of the information, education, and entertainment products that will flow through these worldwide networks. This networked world is changing the way we do business, make goods, and provide services.

Living in a Networked World

Manufacturing

Manufacturing is being transformed from its industrial-age model to one that relies on global networks. Changes are apparent from process to product.

- Customers "custom design" products such as automobiles and clothing, electronically transmitting their requirements to remote locations capable of quickly manufacturing and distributing these products.

- Small- and medium-sized companies advertise their manufacturing capabilities over computer networks and efficiently bid on projects required by other companies.
- "Software system brokers" connect users who have a need for temporary access to sophisticated manufacturing tools that would be too expensive to acquire.
- Manufacturers and suppliers use "intelligent" procurement systems to ease and speed parts procurement, as well as billing and payment transactions, to reduce costs, to improve accuracy, and to meet customer demands.

For example, in building a new facility to manufacture its Saturn cars, General Motors developed an information infrastructure to enable Saturn and its numerous suppliers to operate as one virtual company. Through the implementation of a production scheduling database and the use of electronic data interchange (EDI), Saturn and its suppliers reduced overhead and increased cooperation.

Education is required to conceptualize and execute these improvements. The need goes beyond simply analytical or technical skills to understand what is feasible from a manufacturing point of view. It also requires creative and practical skills that allow employees to see new possibilities and make them happen.

Health care

Most countries face similar challenges in providing health care to their people—spiraling costs and access to good care and information. Networking applications are already being used to help address these challenges.

- Community health care information networks allow physicians, hospitals, patients, and others access to critical health information.
- Desktop videoconference applications allow patients to consult with physicians and specialists at regional and national centers.
- Advanced networks enable full-motion video communication and high-speed transmission of critical medical images, such as x-rays and CAT scans, facilitating consultations with medical experts for both primary diagnoses and second opinions.
- Where hospital care may not be available, or for patients needing long-term care (such as chronically ill children or the elderly), home computers allow patients access to instructions for home treatment and give them access to the expert advice of doctors through e-mail.

Some experts estimate that telecommunications applications could reduce health care costs by between $36 billion and $100 billion each year while improving quality of service and increasing access.

Government

Governments around the world are turning to information processing and networking technologies to solve the dilemma of growing budget deficits, increasing demand for services, and proliferating data that must be collected and processed.

For example, in Singapore, more efficient operations are made possible by integrated port information systems that support the electronic sharing of data and documents: more than 80 percent of port information is handled electronically. TradeNet, a system in operation since 1989, has reduced the processing time for trade documents from an average of two days to 10 minutes and has reduced the number of forms required for a ship to clear the harbor from 20 to one (IBM 1997).

Making it easier and more convenient for people to complete transactions—linking information and experts via the network—has improved the efficiency of many processes. The Colorado Department of Labor has converted eight unemployment offices around the state from traditional counter-based operations to sites supported by computer kiosks. At these locations, an individual can complete an application and search for information directly from the kiosk without having to deal with any paper forms. When there are questions or someone would like to discuss specific job openings, they use the videoconferencing facility at the kiosk to speak with a counselor located in Denver. The kiosks meet the needs of citizens by providing user-friendly access to information as well as expert help. The state benefits by having "at the source" entry of data and by minimizing office space and workforce requirements.

New opportunities

Contrary to fears, technology is not eliminating good jobs. Actually, technology is generating more jobs, especially those requiring problem-solving ability, and those jobs are paying better and better. Where once a teller handled transactions one by one, now a systems analyst upgrades the software for automatic teller machines. There is a growing demand for truck drivers who can use computers and modems to make just-in-time deliveries and for auto technicians who can repair the electronic systems that guide today's cars (Reich 1996). Compensation for IT professionals increases approximately 20 percent each year (ITAA 1997).

One of these new opportunities is electronic commerce. As more commercial and industrial transactions are nationally and internationally linked, electronic commerce networks are emerging. These networks allow a wide variety of transactions to take place:

- a credit card customer pays for a purchase electronically
- a government customs officer enters the amount of customs duty an importer owes electronically
- factories order parts and maintain inventories automatically, as do retailers
- transportation systems are managed electronically, coordinating arrivals, departures, and exchange of baggage on flights

With electronic commerce, the productivity of business transactions within and across nations will be improved. International trade will become more active, with transactions and communications made easier.

Beyond electronic commerce, IT is allowing existing businesses to be reconceptualized; entirely new enterprises are being created. Consider the changes the World Wide Web (WWW) has enabled in the airline industry as just one example. The first step was to allow employee access to information via the Web. Then home pages became accessible to the public. As the business became progressively more Web enabled, flight schedules were posted to the Web and queries could be made. Then, frequent flyer applications were accepted online, followed by the ability to purchase tickets via the Web. Now we have ticketless travel. Technology has enabled new opportunities for the airline industry as well as its customers. Behind the scenes, a multitude of other opportunities and new jobs have emerged. Consultants are needed to create strategies. Webmasters are in demand to create, maintain, and update Web pages. Other experts ensure the security of company and customer data, and others see to the integration of existing systems with a Web front-end.

As a result of technology, entirely new opportunities are being created through the use of customer profiles to tailor standard products. New startups and well-established industry leaders are now offering customized goods and services over the network, collecting valuable customer information as they go. Developing and leveraging a personal profile for each individual customer is an increasingly common strategy.

<Amazon.com> attracts customers with a value proposition that permits access to more than a million titles at lower prices than most book stores. Once inside their Web site, customers can post their own reviews of books, exchange e-mail with their favorite authors, and request electronic alerts about their favorite subjects or authors. Each interaction adds to Amazon's knowledge about individual customers, adds to their growing virtual community, and steadily increases barriers to customer switching vendors.

<GreetSt.com> is a greeting card startup that quickly seized the Internet potential to feature direct access to 20,000 cards, with custom greetings and U.S. Postal Service mailing. Their Personal Memory feature automatically reminds subscribers of key upcoming events and which card was sent last year.

A more complex business model involves the assembly of standardized components into a complete customized offering to meet the specific needs of a single customer. For example, Levi Strauss has created the "Personal Pair." It requires six accurate measurements instead of the traditional two measurements (waist and inseam), and will guarantee that its product provides a perfect fit. Levi saves 75 percent of inventory and distribution costs. At the same time they are able to charge a premium price. Customer satisfaction is outstanding. Customer size dimensions are captured in a database for future orders.

The transformation

All around us we find evidence of tailored products, targeted marketing, and customization. Consumer demand for more choices, higher quality, lower cost, better service, and convenient access points is a dominant force affecting all industries—including higher education.

It is not just that consumers want goods that match their personal preferences; IT has enabled enterprises to understand and meet an increasing variety of consumer needs. Information technology enables firms to meet consumer demands by supporting

- product development for hundreds of thousands of products;
- selection and management of hundreds of micro-market segments;
- efficient administration of millions of client relationships;
- product cycles measured in weeks or months instead of years; and
- direct consumer access through a variety of access points.

Changes in technology, global economics, the increasing value of time, and other customer preferences are causing the alteration of traditional business and industry models. These shifts are evident in the structure of industries, in the barriers to entry, the markets they choose to serve, and the channels for distribution as well as their products.

	FROM	TO
Structure	Vertical integration	Multi-firm value nets
Market entry	Restricted, regulated	Open, deregulated
	High barriers	Low barriers
Markets	Mass market	Micro-market
	Local, regional	Global
Channels	Static channels	Dynamic hybrid channels
	Human intermediaries	Interactivity
	Disintermediation	
	New "infomediaries"	
Products	Standard	Personally tailored
	Narrow choice	Broad choice

In short, IT is changing the structure of business and industry. Businesses are becoming more reliant on complex webs of suppliers and customers, competitors and complementors. Barriers to entry are no longer predominantly physical or financial; putting up a storefront or managing an inventory may no longer be required. Potentially, anyone who can put up a Web page can be in business. We are moving from mass markets to markets of one. Geographic limitations are being transcended; most markets are global. Reaching customers and doing business in a networked world is different.

IMPLICATIONS

Changes in technology will impact business, industry, and education. When coupled with social attitudes, such as the increasing value of time and the recognition that technology can be a competitive differentiator, there are a number of implications for the future.

Relationships Depend on Information Access

Technology enables the transmission of information. But fundamentally, the critical process is people interacting with other people. The world does not run on information; it runs on relationships. However, information enables us to have different relationships.

Information is the currency of exchange in campus relationships. Information is exchanged in the classroom between faculty and students. Information is exchanged among research teams. Information is exchanged between the purchasing department and suppliers. Information is exchanged between college applicants and the admissions department. The potential quantities of information are staggering. But it is how the institution manages the information to form relationships that can yield competitive advantage.

Getting Connected

Another impact of IT will be on the sharing of courses and instructional content. As common formats, increased network bandwidth, and rights management improve, institutions with educational content are increasingly likely to share courses and content. The sharing of authentic or original information brings students closer to the level of scholarship that faculty experience. It is through working with authentic material, coupled with learning the "way of thinking" of a particular scholarly community, that students enhance their learning.

The ability of students to connect with experts around the world, as well as their peers, opens new opportunities for learning and enrichment, as well. Students and faculty find these opportunities motivating. In addition to the uniqueness of the experience, contact with other cultures and with individuals from the workplace tends to broaden cross-cultural awareness and fosters an appreciation of real-world, complex issues with which students will wrestle upon graduation.

Finally, distributed instruction, the explosive growth of networks, and the trend to move bits instead of people and things will continue to erode the geographic hegemony of higher education institutions.

New Media Forms

There are a number of indications that education is wrestling with understanding and validating a new media form. Electronic journals become more common every day, yet they are not considered the equivalent of print journals. Courses offered via the Web do not automatically receive the same number of credits as those offered in a classroom. According to middle school teachers, students are more comfortable writing in hypertext than in a traditional term-paper format. Computer-generated music and computer-generated art are relative newcomers to the academic scene. We are comfortable with authentication procedures, peer review, and quality control mechanisms for familiar media. However, most of us are still unsure how to handle quality control and intellectual property management in a medium where one can be a producer as well as a consumer.

As new media forms rise in importance, others might diminish. Noam (1997) contends that books will decline in importance. Part of the reason is that they are inefficient. He says that visual information is by far and away the fastest way to absorb information. Print takes up only a tiny fraction of our absorptive capacity. We are using hopelessly outmoded Phoenician and Latin alphabet and traditional forms of written languages. What is more likely to happen is that we will shift to a multimedia form of communication with more visual and symbolic information. He predicts that more pictures, symbols, and video clips will be part of what we now call the written language, because this can speed up the absorption process; it combines the abstraction of written language with the speed of visual image for other types of messages.

Although their digital nature makes these media forms different, does it make them bad? These new media and forms of scholarship will likely develop similar to the introduction of the printing press, the radio, or the telephone. Digital media will not replace other media. They will coexist. As Noam asks, "Is it not *knowledge* that we really cherish? A new and creative medium is knocking at the door and we should embrace it" (Noam 1997, 14).

CHANGE IS IMMINENT

Skeptics still question whether technology will have an impact on higher education. Even though many are calling for the transformation of higher education, an equal number see no reason to change. These "traditionalists" often cite how stable higher education has been for hundreds of years. Since the Gutenberg Bible was printed in 1456 using movable type, the technology of information storage, retrieval, and transmission—the university's basic technology—has remained essentially constant until the current era. Indeed, the use of written records to supplement oral teaching goes back to the fifth century B.C.E. Since their inception, universities and colleges have relied upon lectures, discussions, and the written word because these were the only technologies available.

Information technology has opened new, fundamentally different options for higher education, both in how to run "the business of higher education" as well as in teaching and learning. History demonstrates that fundamental technological change ultimately begets significant structural change, regardless of whether the affected participants choose to join or resist the movement. The changes that universities have weathered over the centuries did not upend their basic technology. Information technology does (Massy 1997).

It is revealing to consider the last great shift in information processing—the one from orality to literacy as mediated by the technology of the alphabet. Socrates lamented the destruction of memory by writing. Plato predicted, correctly, the loss of the capacity to memorize large bodies of acoustical material (Miller 1995).

When printing emerged in the late fifteenth century it was not always welcome, either. "Filippo di Strata declared in the late fifteenth century, '...The world has got along perfectly well for six thousand years without printing, and has no need to change now.' Johannes Trithemius, in *In Praise of* printing, and has no need to change now.' Johannes Trithemius, in *In Praise of Scibes*, says, 'Printed books will never be the equivalent of handwritten codices...The simple reason is that copying by hand involves more diligence and industry'" (Noam 1997, 3).

When movies were invented and did not show Shakespeare's plays but vaudeville dancers and even bare ankles, traditionalists sought a ban. Later, when sound was introduced into motion pictures, musicians' unions insisted that sound movies were economic and cultural murder. When the radio arrived, researchers noted that "Parents have become aware of a puzzling change in the behavior of their children...." And the telephone was driving people permanently insane (Noam 1997).

Within the next decade, IT and its effects as a transformation agent will have a dramatic impact on our lifestyles, workstyles, and education. Technology will become ubiquitous. Its presence and power will be taken for granted. This revolution holds great promise and presents great challenges. It will be difficult to manage but impossible to resist.

QUESTIONS TO ASK

- As an institution, do we understand how IT is changing how we work and live? How it is changing how our students work and live?
- How is IT changing the expectations of our students for facilities, services, and support?
- Does our curriculum reflect the changes that have already occurred across disciplines due to IT and the network?
- Does our curriculum prepare students for the new job opportunities that are being created due to IT and networking?
- Are our faculty leading the development and dissemination of new tools and techniques that capitalize on the capability of the Internet to improve the effectiveness and efficiency of products and services?
- Are our faculty and students prepared to help business reconceptualize itself and create new enterprises based on the capabilities of the World Wide Web?
- If IT has caused shifts in the structure of industries, barriers to entry, markets and channels for distribution, how will those same forces affect higher education?
- Are our faculty actively engaged in the exploration of the new media forms made possible by IT? Are they wrestling with how to validate these new media forms?
- Has our institution accepted that change, due to IT, is imminent? What actions have been taken to capitalize on that change?

CHAPTER 5

Global Interdependence

Virtually anything can be made and sold anywhere. Telecommunications and modern transportation systems have created a truly global community. Products can be designed in one place, engineered in another, produced in yet a third, and distributed around the globe. Finance, capital, technology, and labor acknowledge no national borders; neither does education. Since 1992, education has ranked fifth in U.S. cross-border sale of services. In 1994, the United States earned about $7 billion for educational services (Lenn 1997).

Technology and shortened product life cycles, as well as new standards for quality and customer satisfaction, are joined by globalization as major change agents in the economy. Of these, globalization may pose the most difficult adjustment. One impact of globalization is that the United States no longer dominates the world economy. Since World War II the U.S. economy has fallen from 40 percent of the world's output to 22 percent. One in five of the largest companies in the world are now headquartered outside the United States, Japan, Germany, France, and the United Kingdom. In 1972, that figure was one in 10. Perhaps one of the most telling statistics is that 95 percent of the world's consumers live someplace other than the United States. Economic growth is more rapid outside the United States than in this country (Jones 1997a).

SHIFT FROM NATIONAL TO GLOBAL

America's dependence on global trade has grown. Overall, foreign trade now accounts for nearly one-quarter of America's gross domestic product—well over $1 trillion a year (Potter and Youngman 1997).

The world in which most adult Americans grew to maturity no longer exists. The cold war is over. The economy is not domestic; it is global. The "melting pot" is boiling over. Our world is in flux. The approach of the twenty-first century foreshadows not simply a new millennium, but a completely new and different globe (ACE 1995). However, for many of us, our perceptions have not kept pace with reality.

The United States No Longer Dominates the Global Economy

Many of us grew up with an assumption that the United States dominated the world. The truth is that today we are one among many.

- At the end of World War II the U.S. economy represented 40 percent of the world's output; today it represents 22 percent.
- In 1970 the United States accounted for 55 percent of the 500 largest global companies; by 1995, 31 percent of the global 500 called the United States home.
- Of the 18 largest chemical companies in the world, only three are U.S. companies.
- Of the 64 largest commercial banks, only nine are U.S.-based; the five largest commercial banking companies are in other countries.
- Of the 30 leading electronic and electrical equipment manufacturers in the world, only eight are in the United States.
- Of the 11 largest food companies, only five are in the United States.
- Of the 15 largest metal companies, only one is U.S.-based.
- Of the 26 largest motor vehicle and parts manufacturers, only six companies are in the United States (NAB 1997c).

Not only do 95 percent of the world's consumers reside someplace other than the United States, but economic growth is more rapid outside the United States than it is here. For example, in Malaysia it is 4 percent a year, in China it is 8 percent, in South Korea it is 6 percent, in Chile it is 8 percent, and in Ireland it is 5 percent. As these countries experience economic growth, they behave similar to the United States in the 1950s and 1960s (Jones 1997a). The availability of more disposable income makes them better consumers. It also increases the size of the middle class. Believe it or not, there are more middle class individuals in India than in the United States. They will behave very much like we do—only there will be millions more of them than of us.

The growth of earning power in other countries creates jobs for businesses in the United States. They represent new markets. However, as consumers they have options, as well. They may choose to buy from local firms or they may choose to buy from our "foreign" competitors.

International Integration and Interdependence

In the global marketplace, companies, industries, products, technologies, and even jobs no longer depend upon the strengths and weaknesses of any one nation's economy or industrial base. Jobs lost at home reappear abroad. Industrial accidents spread pollution across borders and among trading blocs. American graduates must compete with their peers from overseas. In truth, the line separating "foreign" from "domestic" is much harder to define today than it was yesterday, and much of our "domestic" success depends on events taking place elsewhere (ACE 1995).

In the emerging high-value economy, fewer products have distinct nationalities. Consider some examples.

- Precision ice hockey equipment is designed in Sweden, financed in Canada, and assembled in the United States and Denmark for distribution in North America and Europe, respectively, out of alloys whose molecular structure was researched and patented in the United States and fabricated in Japan.
- A sports car is financed in Japan, designed in Italy, and assembled in the United States, Mexico, and France, using advanced electronic components invented in the United States and fabricated in Japan.
- A microprocessor is designed in the United States and financed in the United States and West Germany, containing dynamic random-access memory fabricated in South Korea.
- A jet airplane is designed in the United States and in Japan, and assembled in the United States with tail cones from Canada, special tail sections from China and Italy, and engines from Britain.
- A space satellite designed in the United States, manufactured in France, and financed by Australians is then launched from a rocket made in the Soviet Union.

Which of these is an American product? Which a foreign product? How does one decide? Perhaps the most relevant question is: Does it matter? (Reich 1991).

Information technologies have integrated university and industry laboratories worldwide, diffusing technological advances at rates unconceived of even a decade ago. With worldwide technology diffusion and simultaneous transmission of information, products themselves are increasingly global. In one product cycle, basic research, process development, safety and quality standards development, basic manufacturing, assembly and/or customization can each occur in a different country, or more than one country (Potter and Youngman 1997).

What is traded among nations is less often finished products than specialized problem-solving, problem-identifying and brokerage services, all of which create value. When an American buys a Pontiac Le Mans from General Motors (GM), for example, he or she engages in an international transaction. Of the $10,000 paid to GM, about $3,000 goes to South Korea for routine labor and assembly operations; $1,750 to Japan for advanced components (engines, transaxles, and electronics); $750 to West Germany for styling and design engineering; $400 to Taiwan, Singapore, and Japan for small components; $250 to Britain for advertising and marketing services; and about $50 to Ireland and Barbados for data processing. The rest—less than $4,000—goes to strategists in Detroit, lawyers and bankers in New York, lobbyists in Washington, insurance and health care workers all over the country, and GM shareholders—most of whom live in the United States, but an increasing number of whom are foreign nationals (Reich 1991).

Beyond these manufacturing and design interdependencies, globalization is having some novel time-based applications. With the rapid movement of information, companies can now take advantage of time zones. A software project can be situated in Silicon Valley at one point during the day, move to Asia for another iteration, and spend the final leg of its 24-hour evolution with a team in Europe. With the pace of change and the enormous competitive pressures to bring innovative products to market faster than the competition, keeping a team working 24 hours a day may become more routine (Kanin-Lovers 1997).

Competition Comes from All Directions

Global competition is one of the most significant forces of change for business in the last decade. Nearly three-quarters of American goods manufactured today are subject to competition from abroad (ACE 1997). Even the smallest company now needs to do business on a worldwide scale. We are facing a host of new competitors, globally. For example, until the late 1970s, AT&T had depended on workers in Shreveport, Louisiana, to assemble standard telephones. It then discovered that firms in Singapore would perform the same tasks at a far lower cost. Facing intense competition, AT&T felt compelled to switch. So in the early 1980s they stopped hiring labor in Shreveport and began hiring cheaper workers in Singapore. But under this kind of pressure for ever lower production costs, today's Singaporean can easily end up in the same circumstances as yesterday's Louisianan. In the late 1980s, AT&T found that employees in Thailand were eager to assemble telephones for a small fraction of the wages of workers in Singapore. Thus, in 1989, AT&T stopped hiring

Singaporeans to make telephones and began hiring workers in Thailand (Reich 1991).

It is tempting to assume that much of this global pressure is due to illiterate workers or exploitative labor practices. In some cases this may be true, but global competition is no longer restricted to opportunities presented by a large, inexpensive unskilled labor pool. Increasingly, competition is coming from educated, highly productive workforces.

Data entry operators located anywhere around the world can enter data into computers and pull that data out again. As the rates charged by satellite networks continue to drop, and as more satellites and fiber-optic cables become available (reducing communication costs still further), routine data processors in the United States find themselves in ever more direct competition with their counterparts abroad, who are often eager to work for far less.

By 1990, data entry operators in the United States were earning, at most, $6.50 per hour. But data entry operators throughout the rest of the world were willing to work for a fraction of this. Thus, many potential American data-processing jobs were disappearing, and the wages and benefits of the remaining ones were in decline. Typical was Saztec International, a $20-million-a-year data-processing firm headquartered in Kansas City, which contracted with data processors in Manila and with American-owned firms that needed such data- processing services. Compared with the average Philippine income of $1,700 per year, data-entry operators working for Saztec earned the princely sum of $2,650 (Reich 1991).

By 1990, American Airlines was employing more than 1,000 data processors in Barbados and the Dominican Republic to enter names and flight numbers from used airline tickets (flown daily to Barbados from airports around the United States) into a giant computer bank located in Dallas. Chicago publisher R. R. Donnelley was sending entire manuscripts to Barbados for entry into computers in preparation for printing. The New York Life Insurance Company was dispatching insurance claims to Castle Island, Ireland, where workers, guided by simple directions, entered the claims and determined the amounts due, then instantly transmitted the computations back to the United States. And McGraw-Hill was processing subscription renewal and marketing information for its magazines in nearby Galway. Indeed, literally millions of workers around the world are receiving information, converting it into computer-readable form, and then sending it back—at the speed of electronic impulses—whence it came (Reich 1991).

With work depending more on information than raw materials or energy, as was the case in the industrial era, developing countries have new opportunities for growth and development. The strategy of many countries is to skip over being an industrial power and move directly to being a power broker in the information age. It is a savvy approach for many. For those with massive populations, their raw power is in people. If they are educated, have a strong work ethic, and are motivated to become middle-class consumers, they will become fierce competitors with the United States and Western Europe. This is the strategy of an increasing number of developing nations.

In addition to the massive population base and their desire to improve their economic standing, these countries appear to be more willing to make decisions and allocate resources to education than many developed nations. The potential benefits of IT, telecommunications, and education are enormous in these countries and their politicians realize it. They have little to lose. With modest investments in existing infrastructure, these countries' emerging networks—connecting and processing data and images in all forms—can help them leapfrog technological handicaps, thereby accelerating economic development and advancing social progress. Many developing nations are planning to do just that. Will we be able to maintain our edge in infrastructure or education? Are our institutions the leaders?

Many developing nations also have designed economic policies that attract outside investors to an information-based workforce. If you believe that multimedia, visualization, and other technologies are the wave of the future, there is every reason to believe that these countries will be strong competitors.

The United States is not the only country concerned with global competitiveness. In a report focused on Europe, concerns very similar to ours are expressed: "Technology has introduced far-reaching changes to economic and social life, with perhaps the greatest impact in the workplace. This poses enormous challenges for Europe to adapt to a global marketplace and retain a competitive edge. The acquisition of skills for the new types of employment which are being created will be a critical factor in our success; we need to become a 'Learning Society' " (IBM 1996, 1).

Redefining Success in Business

"By the 1990s, the ownership of many American corporations had moved outside our borders—RCA, BS Records, American Can, Columbia Pictures, Doubleday, Mack Truck, Allis-Chalmers, Firestone, Goodyear, Giant Food, Pillsbury, and National Steel. The list seemed to grow longer by the day. And as it grew, many Americans became increasingly concerned. . . . Such concerns, however, are the product of outmoded thinking. They are based on a picture of national corporations and industries that is no longer accurate. As corporations of all nations are transformed into global webs, the important question—from the standpoint of national wealth—is not which nation's citizens own what, but which nation's citizens learn how to do what, so they are capable of adding more value to the world economy and therefore increasing their own potential worth" (Reich 1991, 136–37).

As economies have become more interconnected globally, our definitions of balance and success in business are shifting. Consider the auto industry. Beginning in 1991, Japan's Mazda began producing Ford Probes at Mazda's plant in Michigan. Some of these cars would be exported to Japan and sold there under Ford's trademark. A Mazda-designed compact utility vehicle would be built at a Ford plant in Kentucky and then sold at Mazda dealerships in the United States. Nissan, meanwhile, was designing a new light truck in its California design center. The trucks would be assembled at Ford's Ohio truck plant, using panel parts fabricated by Nissan at its Tennessee factory, and then marketed by both Ford and Nissan in the United States and Japan. Who is Ford? Nissan? Mazda (Reich 1991)?

The structure of business and industry has fundamentally changed. It is no longer a monolithic structure but a global web—highly interconnected and interdependent. For countries like the United States, the focus is on *high-value* not *high-volume* production. American-owned firms, British-owned firms, or Japanese-owned firms will continue making things abroad or contracting with foreigners to supply them with particular goods and services. Those intent on improving the nation's balance of trade would best focus on how to add value in a way that this planet's 5 billion other people cannot.

Accepting Globalization

Globalization represents a structural change. When a structural change occurs, things never go back to the way they were. We will never be able to re-create the time when the United States was the dominant economic force. Globalization is inexorable. Not only can it not be reversed, it cannot be legislated away. Those businesses and organizations that have accepted globalization and understand it are learning how to create an American success model within it. Not outside of it. One of our educational challenges is to integrate globalization into the curriculum in a meaningful way so that we can capitalize on—rather than be constrained by—globalization.

IMPLICATIONS FOR EMPLOYEES

Today, even the smallest company needs to do business on a global scale. Borders are gone. Having a conference, placing an order, or getting information—worldwide—is just a few keystrokes away.

Economic growth will raise the living standards of more people in more parts of the world than at any prior time in history. In the past three years world economic growth was nearly double that of the prior two decades. Such growth and development creates opportunity. But it also creates a challenge. Emerging economies are cultivating a talented and skilled global workforce—one that is vying for historically American jobs.

One U.S.-based insurance company is sending much of its claim reimbursement work to its office in Ireland. Ireland has one of the highest percentages of college graduates in Western Europe. The company takes its pick of English-speaking graduates, hires, and trains them. Their savings are 35 percent in costs over operations in the United States. And many major IT companies—IBM, Motorola, Texas Instruments—are outsourcing software development to the graduates of the Indian Institute of Science in Bangalore, which produces world-class programmers (Verville 1996).

The trend is for U.S. companies to open offices in places like India and Ireland. Even though you may never have heard of the University of Limerick or the Institute of Science in Bangalore, corporate recruiters have. And often, highly skilled workers overseas are willing to work for less than their American counterparts.

Jobs in the global marketplace are no longer "domestic," no matter on whose turf. Although American jobs may be performed on American soil, they are not dependent solely on the American economy, on the skills of American workers, or on the competitiveness of the American employer. Rather, American jobs increasingly depend upon global economic conditions and global market forces far beyond the reach of American policy makers, employers, or employees. In the new global marketplace, employees' job security is tied to their company's performance in the global marketplace and their own performance in their company (Potter and Youngman 1997).

One impact of globalization is that business must adapt quickly to stay competitive. The rapidly changing needs of employers will require individuals to adapt their skills. As second and third careers become more common, it will be imperative that we see new careers as opportunities to reorient ourselves through retraining. Almost any imaginable scenario makes the ability to continuously learn a critical skill. For many, the type of learning required will be very different from that needed in a mass-production economy where the simplification of tasks and the standardization of technology and production limited the amount of learning needed or achieved. More learning is required in a dynamic, technology-intensive workplace, and more of that learning must be done through the manipulation of abstract symbols. For line workers, mass-production systems stressed learning by observation and doing.

IMPLICATIONS FOR THE CURRICULUM

Many regard globalization as the defining feature of the late twentieth century. If so, it should be reflected in the curriculum. All too often "globalizing your curriculum" is tantamount to requiring two years of a foreign language. American higher education needs to organize itself to educate students for competence and success in an interdependent world. The nation must commit itself now to providing all students with the kinds of knowledge it once provided to only a few—a powerful, deep-rooted understanding of other languages, diverse cultures, and global issues. This kind of competence needs to be provided not as something extra in the curriculum, but as an integral part of the educational experience (ACE 1995).

With English well established as the dominant language of business, can we feel safe? Are we deluding ourselves that requiring two or four years of a foreign language is adequate preparation for the global economy? Where in the curriculum do we address global economics or cultural empathy? How many students forget the geography they learned in middle school because they never use it?

Twenty years ago we were concerned with our curricula reflecting diversity. With the addition of Women's Studies and programs on African literature or Eastern culture, is that job done? Where in the curriculum are our students exposed to the history of Singapore? Of Albania? Of Haiti? Who teaches the philosophy of oriental cultures? What of the political systems of Africa?

Those who travel internationally will report that professionals from other cultures often know much more about us and our political systems than we do about theirs. Americans touring abroad during the past presidential election typically found that their international counterparts knew more about what happened on the campaign trail that day than they did. Aside from making the Americans appear to be out of touch, this is bad for business. One is much more likely to appear an interested and desirable business partner if one knows something about the politics and history of a country when one steps off the plane.

Beyond history, culture, and language, we should ask if the economics taught in higher education prepares graduates for the world of international commerce in which we are engaged. With the rapid, seamless movement of goods, services, and currency around the world, does the eighteenth century mercantile model have direct applicability, or should it be considered a topic more appropriate for the history of economics than the core curriculum?

In fact, changes are underway. Teacher education in global and international education is now mandated by the National Council for Accreditation of Teacher Education (NCATE). Mingling content from fields such as international relations and area/international studies, world history, earth science, and cultural/ethnic studies, students are encouraged to understand the complexity of globalization and develop skills in cross-cultural interaction (Merryfield 1995).

Similar needs have been identified in business education. There is nearly universal agreement that there is an increased need for global knowledge on the part of firms and their managers. Certainly, all business graduates will be affected by international aspects of business. In fact, many business graduates will become involved in international business later in their careers. Managers will need to move away from parochial thinking and develop a depth of knowledge in history, politics, literature, arts, culture, religion, and language—in addition to functional business disciplines (Cavusgil 1993).

An American Council on Education (ACE) report (1995) stresses the importance of students developing the competence to function effectively in a global environment. They propose several ground rules for internationalizing institutions.

- **Require that all graduates demonstrate competence in at least one foreign language.** The ability to use language to interact and work productively with people from other cultures is what institutions should focus on—not the number of courses taken or seat time. Education must become truly international, not simply European. Our institutions confer 10 times as many degrees in German as in Chinese, graduate 18 times as many French speakers as Japanese speakers, and count nearly 500 graduates fluent in Spanish for every one fluent in Arabic.
- **Encourage understanding of at least one other culture.** The educational experience must be infused with some degree of *intercultural competence,* including language competence. All undergraduates need exposure to other peoples, languages, and cultures. This is as true for community college students as it is for those enrolled in liberal arts institutions or state colleges and universities.

  There are any number of ways this can be accomplished—intensive study on campus, study abroad, drawing on the experiences of foreign students on our campuses, internships with trade missions in the United States, electronic bulletin boards, or telecommunications links with institutions in other countries. In the world of the twenty-first century, familiarity with other languages, other cultures, other customs, and other peoples will be the hallmark of the genuinely well-educated person.
- **Increase understanding of global systems.** Graduates need an understanding of *global systems.* Once, only experts needed to understand the dynamics of the international economy—or the interactions among environmental and economic systems or public health. Today these relationships are too important to be left to experts alone. Every day, these global systems affect the quality of the nation's life as exchange rates raise and lower the price of goods and as pollution and public health problems transcend national boundaries. Higher education must develop *problem-focused programs of study* that are more practical than theoretical and that are oriented

around problems in the real world. These new lines of inquiry should explicitly encourage faculty and students to explore issues from a variety of disciplinary and cultural perspectives.

Economic, meteorological, agricultural, and other systems interact with one another in complex and subtle ways. The collapse of the Mexican peso affects not only trade and foreign assistance, but also immigration and health. The disappearance of the rain forests in Brazil would affect climate throughout the world, and could well lead to the extinction of plants that might have been the basis for new medicines.

- **Revamp curricula to reflect the need for international understanding.** Institutions need to (a) develop strategies to help students attain the competence required, (b) set institutional goals for developing required levels of expertise, and (c) clearly state in course catalogs how each course (including study or work abroad) meets these requirements.

- **Expand study abroad and internship opportunities for all students.** Firsthand experience with other peoples, languages, and cultures is an essential complement to formal study. Study and internships abroad are valuable educational experiences. When not possible, however, experiences with other cultures in the United States are helpful.

- **Focus on faculty development and rewards.** In internationalizing education, institutional leaders should not ignore the opportunity to send signals through the faculty development and rewards process. Encourage faculty to develop expertise in the global dimensions of their disciplines. Encourage interdisciplinary study. Give weight to international experience, skill, and foreign language competence as criteria in hiring new faculty. Include international service or study among the criteria for tenure or promotion.

- **Examine the organizational needs of international education.** Does the institution offer adequate support for international students and for its own students to study and work abroad? Are library resources adequate to support an internationalized curriculum? Is the institution making effective use of available technology to expand the resources available to students and faculty?

- **Build consortia to enhance capabilities.** Institutions can encourage excellence in programs and student choice among diverse offerings by entering into consortia and cooperative efforts with other institutions.

- **Cooperate with institutions in other countries.** By definition, international education is a two-way street. The best programs in

American colleges and universities almost inevitably will be those that establish partnerships of one kind or another with institutions in other countries.

- **Work with local schools and communities.** Higher education's public service role requires that institutions work with their local communities, states, and regions—and with local schools—to advance the agenda for change. It is never too early to start learning a second language or exploring foreign cultures. Colleges and universities train the teachers employed in public schools. Teacher training programs should include international and foreign language competence as a condition for graduation and certification. In addition, colleges and universities should routinely offer seminars and forums on international issues for the community, and should work with local economic development agencies to remind community leaders and employers of the international dimensions of modern work and economic development.

IMPLICATIONS FOR THE PROFESSORIATE

In terms of numbers, American universities are more international than ever, educating 450,000 students from other countries and employing staff members from around the world. At the same time, a recent Carnegie survey notes that the American professoriate is least committed to internationalism among scholars from 14 countries. Only half of American faculty feel that connections with scholars in other countries are very important, and while more than 90 percent of faculty in 13 other countries believe that a scholar must read books and journals published abroad to keep up with scholarly developments, only 62 percent of Americans are of this opinion.

American faculty are similarly unenthusiastic about internationalizing the curriculum. Fewer than half agree that the curriculum should be more international. Americans travel abroad for research and study less frequently than do their counterparts in other countries. The Carnegie data show that 65 percent of American academics did not go abroad for study or research in the past three years. This compares with 25 percent of Swedes, 47 percent of Britons, and just 7 percent of Israelis. At the same time, American professors have much more contact with international students than do faculty in other countries—96 percent indicate that foreign students are enrolled at their institutions (Altbach and Maassen 1997).

American faculty seem to feel that U.S. higher education is at the center of an international academic system. The world comes to the United States and therefore international initiatives are superfluous. American academics do not often cite work by scholars in other countries in their research. The

American research system is remarkably insular, especially when compared to scientific communities in other countries (Altbach and Maassen 1997).

With teaching, learning, scholarship, and service highly dependent on the experience base and attitudes of the professoriate, it may be difficult for globalization to penetrate higher education. As the Carnegie study concluded, academics seem to have little consciousness of the external forces affecting colleges and universities. There is a strong contrast between the substantial impact of globalization on business and industry and its relatively minor role in higher education.

QUESTIONS TO ASK

- Is there a comprehensive institutional strategy for internationalization? Can the strategy be translated into action?
- Is internationalization adopted as a legitimate institutional goal and is it reflected in the mission? Is it reflected in funding priorities?
- Have instructional materials been prepared or acquired to support a globalization of the curriculum?
- Are there international professional development opportunities available for faculty?
- Does the merit system recognize and reward internationalization efforts in teaching, research, and service?
- Are there overseas study opportunities for students? Are international internships available?
- What meaningful linkages with business and industry would promote globalizing the curriculum? Are there beneficial linkages with other colleges and universities?

PART THREE

· · · · · · · · · · · ·

What We Will Need

CHAPTER 6

What Business Needs

Business is highly competitive. Being good enough today is no guarantee of surviving tomorrow. In many respects, there are new rules governing business. As business changes, jobs change. As jobs change, the type of graduates needed by business changes. With the rapid changes in new technology, the existence of global economies, and the approaching dominance of niche marketing, business needs people who can deal with change and be effective.

SUCCESSFUL INTELLIGENCE

Business needs people who are "successfully intelligent." Sternberg (1996) contends that successfully intelligent people think well in three different ways: analytically, creatively, and practically. In addition, the three aspects of successful intelligence are related. Analytical thinking is required to solve problems and to judge the quality of ideas. Creative intelligence is required to formulate good problems and ideas in the first place. Practical intelligence is needed to use the ideas and their analysis in an effective way, whether in business or in everyday life. Balance is important, as well. It is more important to know when and how to use these aspects of successful intelligence than just to have them.

The dilemma is that educational organizations appear to value analytical intelligence above all else. Unfortunately, the style of intelligence most readily recognized as "smart" (analytical intelligence) may well be less useful to many students in their working lives than creative and practical intelligence. In this respect, we may mislead and misprepare students by developing and rewarding a set of skills that will be much less important later in life than they were in school. Education needs to be preparing students to live in a world where what matters is successful intelligence, not just inert, analytical intelligence (Sternberg 1996).

Whether it is taught in schools, colleges, or universities, successful intelligence is required in business. Many executives complain that too many top-level graduates of business schools are good at analyzing textbook cases of business problems but are unable to come up with innovative ideas for new business products or services, or ways to stay competitive with similar industries in other countries. The point is that there are large gaps between the kind of performance needed for success in a business setting and the kind required for success in schools, even those that attempt to be quite practical in training students for the world of business. The result is that we often end up with adults who are unable to do what is expected of them in a work setting (Sternberg 1996).

The emphasis on analytical intelligence is not wrong, just unbalanced. A company like Intel succeeds partially because of innovation. As one product is being introduced to the market, its successor is already being developed. So, as other companies scramble to catch up, Intel is already moving ahead of them, maintaining its position as a market leader. Analytical intelligence is important in knowing the market for any product, but creative intelligence is what produces products in the first place and keeps them coming out (Sternberg 1996).

Analytical intelligence is most comparable to the facts, figures, and reasoning taught in our education system. Creativity, although not easy to define, is a well-recognized concept. Practical intelligence is the aspect of successful intelligence that helps people adapt to their environments, e.g., learning how the system works. It is similar to "*street* smarts." There is more required for success in life than "*school* smarts." Although estimates vary, only 4–25 percent of the variation in job performance is accounted for by cognitive-ability test scores. An academically intelligent individual may lack the ability to know how to do things and the capacity to get them done.

Sternberg provides several definitions of what it means to be successfully intelligent. His list provides useful guidelines for many of the capabilities business needs from employees.

- Successfully intelligent people are flexible in adapting to the roles they need to fulfill. They recognize that they will have to change the way they work to fit the task and situation at hand, and then they analyze what these changes will have to be and make them.

- Successfully intelligent people don't wait for problems to hit them over the head; they recognize their existence before they get out of hand and begin the process of solving them.
- Successfully intelligent people define problems correctly and thereby solve those problems that really confront them, rather than extraneous ones. In this way, the same problems don't keep coming back into their lives. They also make the effort to decide which problems are worth solving in the first place, and which aren't.
- Successfully intelligent people carefully formulate strategies for problem solving. In particular, they focus on long-range planning rather than rushing in and then later having to rethink their strategies.
- Successfully intelligent people think carefully about allocating resources, for both the short term and the long term. They consider the risk-reward ratios and then choose the allocations they believe will maximize their return.
- Successfully intelligent people do not always make the correct decisions, but they monitor and evaluate their decisions and then correct their errors as they discover them.
- Successfully intelligent people think heuristically to solve problems. Faced with a problem, they analyze it carefully and then use creative strategies to find a solution.

ATTRIBUTES OF GRADUATES

Both academics and employers complain that college graduation requirements, based primarily on passing sets of courses, fail to ensure that the graduate has the personal qualities and skills needed to succeed in graduate school, professional training, or in the workplace. These skills include initiative, persistence, integrity, the ability to communicate effectively, to think creatively as well as critically, and to work with others to solve problems. "Many educators will claim that our colleges already provide just such preparation. But if we listen to those who employ our graduates or to educators in graduate and professional schools, we hear that an enormous chasm exists between what higher education claims it is doing and what is actually achieved" (Langenberg 1997, A64).

Successful employees need the knowledge, skills, and personal attitudes that will enable them to work in the present as well as the future organization.

Several attributes pertaining to the individual, himself or herself, play an important role in the ability of graduates to fit into the work culture, to do the job, develop ideas, take initiative and responsibility, and ultimately help organizations deal with change. These personal attributes include:

- intellect, ranging from analysis, critique, and synthesis to problem solving

- knowledge, both real and potential, ranging from an understanding of the basic principles of a subject or discipline to knowledge of the organization and commercial awareness—in many organizations knowledge of a subject is less important than the ability to acquire knowledge
- willingness and ability to learn and continue learning throughout life
- flexibility and adaptability to respond to change, to anticipate change, and to lead change
- self-management skills, such as self-discipline, ability to deal with stress, prioritization, planning, and an ability to juggle several things at once
- self-motivation, ranging from being a self-starter to seeing things through to a conclusion, including such characteristics as resilience, tenacity, and determination
- positive self-image, including self-confidence, self-awareness, self-belief, self-sufficiency, self-direction, and self-promotion (Harvey et al. 1997)

Although individual attributes are important, they are only part of what is needed. Also required are those attributes involving interaction among people such as interpersonal skills, teamwork, and communication skills. These include the ability to

- communicate, formally and informally, with a wide range of people both internal and external to the organization;
- relate to, and feel comfortable with, people at all levels in the organization as well as a range of external stakeholders and to be able to make and maintain relationships as circumstances change; and
- work effectively in teams—often more than one team at once—and to be able to readjust roles from one project situation to another in an ever-shifting work environment (Harvey et al. 1997).

SKILLS FOR THE FLEXIBLE ORGANIZATON

Teamwork, communication, and interpersonal skills are inextricably linked in the flexible organization; they are attributes of those who are successfully intelligent. For instance, it is highly unlikely that someone with underdeveloped interpersonal skills would be able to engage effectively with colleagues and clients, let alone inspire a team. Being a good communicator, having well-developed interpersonal skills, being an effective team player, and having an understanding of the culture enable the employee to "fit in" to the organization.

Changes in the work environment are leading to the creation of the flexible organization. Flexible organizations require employees and managers with different skills than those of yesterday's more rigid, hierarchical organizations.

Changes in the work environment are leading to the creation of the flexible organization. Flexible organizations require employees and managers with different skills than those of yesterday's more rigid, hierarchical organizations.

CHARACTERISTICS OF THE NEW WORLD OF WORK AND THE OLD

Traditional Work	High-Performance Work

Markets

Traditional Work	High-Performance Work
Limited competition	Global competition
Standardization	Customization
Unlimited resources	Limited resources
Regulation	Deregulation

Corporate Characteristics

Traditional Work	High-Performance Work
Mass production	Small lots
Hierarchies	Teams
Large bureaucratic organizations	Smaller flexible organizations
Integrated companies	Outsourcing
Homogeneous workforce	Diverse workforce

Employee Implications

Traditional Work	High-Performance Work
Brawn/metal-bending	Brains/mind-bending
Job security through seniority	Job security through skills
Job-specific skills	Broad skills
Careers built with one employer	Careers built in one occupation
Benefits tied to employer	Portable benefits
Pay for time served	Pay for performance
Finite education	Lifelong learning

Source: American Council on Education (ACE). 1997. Spanning the chasm: Corporate and academic cooperation to improve work force preparation. Task Force on High Performance Work and Workers: The Academic Connection, Washington, 14.

Initially, employers want *adaptive* employees, people who can adapt to the organization, understand the job requirements, and produce work that has a clear return—as quickly as possible. Adding value, especially in the short term, relies on knowledge, speed of learning, ability to work in teams, and adjusting to the culture of the organization (Harvey et al. 1997).

In the long term, however, employees need to move along a continuum from being adaptive to exerting a transformative influence on their environment.

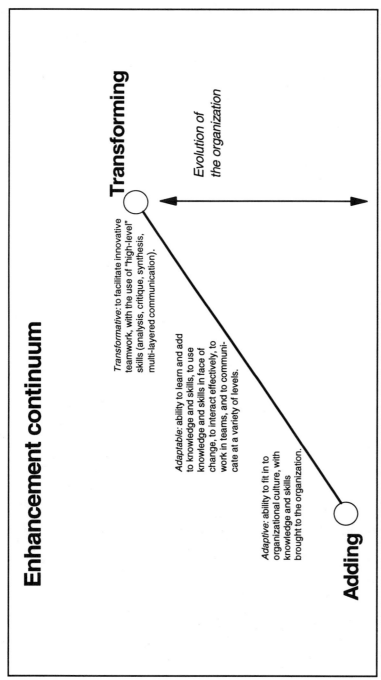

Enhancement continuum

Transforming

Evolution of
the organization

Transformative: to facilitate innovative
teamwork, with the use of "high-level"
skills (analysis, critique, synthesis,
multi-layered communication).

Adaptable: ability to learn and add
to knowledge and skills, to use
knowledge and skills in face of
change, to interact effectively, to
work in teams, and to communicate at a variety of levels.

Adaptive: ability to fit in to
organizational culture, with
knowledge and skills
brought to the organization.

Adding

Source: Harvey, Lee, Sue Moon, and Vicki Geall. 1997. *Graduates' Work: Organizational Change and Students' Attributes.* Birmingham, England: Centre for Research into Quality, the University of Central England, 22.

What most employers want are people who can get to the start of this continuum quickly—add value from the beginning—and have the potential to move up the continuum rapidly, helping to transform their organization. Flexible organizations need people who can take their organization forward and who see change as an opportunity, not a threat. They want *transformative agents* who can help the organization evolve (Harvey et al. 1997).

Transformative agents, by definition, have ideas, "think outside the box," cause friction, and look ahead. People who can transform organizations have the ability to apply their intellectual skills—analysis, critique, and synthesis—to steer change. Such people can see new possibilities and are prepared to take risks and push the boundaries to effect change. These people can lead, develop, and motivate their teams. These transformative agents never stop learning (Harvey et al. 1997).

WORLD OF WORK AND CORPORATE CULTURE

There is a strong move in business and industry to focus on client value as the best way to increase real and potential business revenue. The obsession is on delivering what is of value to the client, not necessarily what is of value to the producer. This requires learning as much as possible about the client. Throughout projects, the client is continually consulted, questioned, and challenged. This involves pushing down to the root cause of a problem, understanding what the client wants to achieve. Higher education rarely prepares students for this objective problem-solving role. In fact, the notion of "customer" is actively resisted by many in higher education.

When asked, employees stress the need for a more serious and comprehensive introduction to the demands of the work world. They typically suggest more sustained attention to the "nuts and bolts" of corporate life, including an introduction to its politics and norms as well as an overview of the personal behaviors expected in it. Many call for more work opportunities. If these are not available, the use of more case studies and team-building activities would be an improvement over the status quo (ACE 1997).

Business leaders, higher education representatives, and recently employed alumni agree that extracurricular experiences add significantly to a student's undergraduate education. These activities, as well as internships, cooperative education experiences, and apprenticeships, enable students to learn skills valued by employers. Interviewees also stressed the need to use group work and case studies within the classroom to teach students how to apply theory to real-world situations (ACE 1997).

MIX SKILLS WITH BROAD EDUCATION

In ACE's study on what business thinks of college graduates, corporate leaders explained that today's college graduates are impressive—in most cases technically as good as or better than their predecessors—but that they are not well qualified to lead in the workplace. It is not that today's graduates are less skilled than those of previous generations, but that expectations for performance are much higher today than ever before. One aspect of these raised expectations is that graduates need not only a broad education but specific skills, as well.

Education versus Training

In discussions of how higher education might improve, it seems inevitable that a debate will emerge between education and training. There is no clear dividing line between education and training nor is there a clear distinction in who should provide which. Whether the mission of higher education is defined as preparation of the mind or preparation for careers, part of that preparation will be education, part will be training. In fact, employees suggest that their education would have been more useful if their colleges had done a better job teaching skills needed in the work world (ACE 1997).

Some experts assert that the more desirable graduates have a liberal arts education, coupled with specific courses in technology—a mix of education and training. Others note that many of the highest salaries are associated with technical specialties; high technology skills are required for a high technology economy. Irrespective of whether a liberal or technical education is chosen, the truth is, a degree may not lead to labor market success. Many curricula represent isolated silos of information. Graduates need to understand the relationship of their chosen disciplines and their work to the broader world.

Systems Perspective

One of the problems cited about graduates is that they cannot see the "big picture." Virtually everything is a system. We must provide our students with the context—a proper view of the whole system—within which our disciplines are practiced. This context likely includes an integrated knowledge of sociology, economics, history, political science, and psychology as well as the legal and ethical aspects of our professions.

Problem Solving

Although we talk about multiple careers, in many respects we have only one: problem solving. The specifics vary with the job, but almost all professional jobs are problem-solving experiences. Perhaps the first job requires solving a mathematical problem. At another point in one's career it might be a financial management problem or a personnel problem. Being able to take an unstructured problem and solve it is the common denominator in many professional careers. Higher education needs to develop problem-solving skills in learners. In addition to understanding the framework for problem solving, students must receive ample opportunities to wrestle with problems of many types—mathematical, sociological, abstract, tangible, realistic, and futuristic.

Integrate Skills into the Curriculum

In addition to problem solving, many core competencies can be built into required courses. Writing and speaking assignments, activities involving small groups and teams, as well as the use of computer skills, are instructional techniques that can be introduced or expanded upon in almost every course. The sequence of instruction will be important and pedagogy will need to change. To learn a problem-solving technique is one thing; to apply it throughout the semester in a political science or sociology course is a far more effective learning strategy. It is one that requires ingenuity on the part of faculty members (Diamond 1997, 69).

Using Information Technology

In most organizations the basic use of IT for such things as word processing and data processing is becoming a more common requirement of graduates: "...they need to be able to access both internal and external databases and networks around the world to gain the latest ideas from the Internet, from academic institutions. They need to be able to build networks, and that requires give and take, communication skills and IT skills, and, slightly to our surprise, we find that a lot of graduates do not have the IT skills that we might now expect of today's generation" (Harvey et al. 1997, 69).

In fact, technology is becoming a required competency in the workplace; it has become another basic skill. Approximately 65 percent of all workers in the United States use some type of IT in their jobs. And estimates are that this number will increase to 95 percent by 2000 (Verville 1995).

Knowledge about the use of technology is required for most employees to remain productive and valuable. Perhaps responding to this trend, educators are now identifying technology-related competencies their graduates need:

- familiarity with and understanding of the roles of technology in the world
- working knowledge of PCs and common software tools
- ability to search, retrieve, analyze, and use electronic information
- mastery of technological applications relevant to their professions and disciplines
- capacity to use technology independently and collaboratively in their work (Hall 1995)

COMMUNICATION

Communication is a major issue for business. What one says and how one says it matters. Although this has always been true, it becomes even more critical with the introduction of self-managed work teams that must routinely make decisions and solve problems on their own. In addition, it is now common for employees to regularly communicate with a range of people beyond their work group, including customers, vendors, and others within the company. It is not just with whom but also what is communicated that has changed. Communication with supervisors, coworkers, and external customers has become more complex because the subjects about which workers are communicating are becoming more complex.

Not all are prepared for the level and kinds of communication required in the workplace. For example, communicating as a member of a team can be different from employee-manager communication. The ability to work from home or a remote location can require a different set of communication skills, as well.

Written Communication

Writing for a variety of audiences is a skill requirement in business. However, while graduates may be proficient at producing essays, laboratory reports, academic projects, and dissertations, they are seen as relatively poor at producing other forms of written communication (Harvey et al. 1997). Much of the correspondence in business is short, succinct, and easy to scan. Action items stand out from background information. Different styles must be adopted for different purposes, as well as for different audiences.

E-mail, the Internet, and Web pages represent new forms of written communication with which students must be facile. An inappropriate comment on e-mail or the wrong distribution list can be career limiting. Although more and more students are exposed to e-mail and other forms of electronic communication, can they tell which represent effective means of communicating? Do they know why? Can they use this communication medium effectively? The assumption is that colleges and universities have a role to play in the development of this competency. However, have faculty had the opportunity to develop their own skills in this area prior to teaching students?

Oral Communication

There is a growing emphasis in business on the need to have good oral communication skills. The expectation is that employees will interact on a personal level with a range of people within a company varying from one-to-one interactions to formal presentations to team discussions to debates.

Messages will go beyond conveying information or instructions to giving praise or reprimands.

For example, there is a substantial element of persuasion necessary in business, industry, education, and daily life. Persuading others moves beyond possessing ideas and views and sharing them. It means being able to convince others that your ideas have worth and persuading them to adopt an idea. This involves clear expression, whether the communication is informal or in a presentation. It also means being able to think on one's feet and coping with critical questions. Styles may need to range from serious to humorous. Of course, the other important side of communication is listening.

Negotiation

Communication is more than speaking, writing, listening, and even persuasion. An often overlooked communication skill is negotiation. Whether in business or in personal life, the ability to negotiate positive outcomes is a significant differentiator. Strong communication skills are only part of negotiating. Another critical factor is being able to identify the real issue and a strategy for approaching the topic. Developing a negotiation strategy involves asking questions such as:

- What are our overall strategic objectives?
- What decisions do I want him or her to make? What do I want? What does he or she want?
- What are the facts? What other information do I need? What are my assumptions? How good are my estimates, assumptions, and facts?
- What are the most and least important issues?
- What is going for or against me on each issue (Karrass 1974)?

Negotiation implies one can ask and listen to determine what the other person thinks or how that person perceives the issue. After one understands the other person's position, one can explain one's own, finding common ground.

TEAMWORK

Whether in the lab or in the office, business and industry value people who know how to work collaboratively; people who can work with colleagues on a problem or a new product, operating in cross-functional teams. These teams need to be increasingly diverse—not just ethnically diverse, but globally diverse. People from all cultures and all countries will need to be able to effectively function as teams in the global market. It is the exception rather than the rule that higher education teaches students how to work in teams.

The autonomous culture of higher education may even work against developing these skills.

Teams involve individuals who work with others and who possess complementary skills. They are committed to a common purpose for which they hold themselves mutually accountable. Teamwork requires a clear understanding of the roles and responsibilities within the group as well as a high level of mutual trust and cooperation. Traditionally, rewards have been based more on individual accomplishment than team goals, and individual competition is more deeply ingrained than mutual accomplishment. This will make the transition to teamwork challenging. However, teams provide a more creative way of solving problems—each member of the team can bring his or her own unique expertise to the situation.

Among the most important characteristics of today's high-performance workplace is the ability to work effectively in teams. No one person has all the competencies needed to create and deliver the complex solutions required by clients and customers. Whether in the laboratory or in the office, business values people who know how to work collaboratively—people who can operate in cross-functional teams of engineers, marketers, lawyers, accountants, and other skilled professionals. "Team hopping," or the ability to move from team to team, is important as well.

Teams are quite different from committees—their conversations and actions focus on the objectives of the group, not on the personal objectives of the individual members. Teams organize themselves and determine roles and ground rules for working together, recognizing that effectiveness hinges on both the task (the problems involved in getting the job done) as well as the process (how the group works as a unit). Effective teams are often characterized by sharing an understanding of what they are trying to do and where the team is going, both in general and in terms of specific objectives. When the team is working well, people can express themselves openly and confront mistakes, confusion, or frustration. For feedback to be received without damaging the cohesion and effectiveness of the team requires mutual support and the development of trust. So obvious that it might be overlooked, teams also have sound procedures that range from calling of meetings and establishing agendas to making decisions.

Teams demand more of employees than does a job in the traditional hierarchical organization. Although the hierarchical organization does not necessarily give the person on the top more power, it does protect subordinates by allowing them to define their "jobs." As long as employees perform their assigned duties they can say, "I did my job," and that is where their responsibility stops. On the other hand, teams require discipline from each member of the team—at all times. Everyone has to work toward the team goals and everyone has to accept the team results (IBM 1990).

Just as teams represent a new role for managers as well as employees, managers now become the team leaders, the communicators with customers, with employees, with peers, and with upper management. Many of the skills required for today's managers depend heavily on teamwork.

- Resource management: finding and assigning skills needed to fulfill the departmental mission
- Developing talent: helping employees get the training needed, developing teaming skills, and helping teams learn to be productive
- Coaching: "pointing the way" for employees, mentoring employees
- Communications: understanding the overall business picture, and how one's department fits into that mission; motivating the entire team to contribute to the business' goals

Can we prepare students for these managerial roles? How do we help those who are now entering management to develop these skills?

Unfortunately, the solitary work and individual competitiveness found on most campuses works at cross-purposes with the cooperation and teamwork expected in the corporate world (ACE 1997). Teamwork is often not part of the academy's modus operandi; autonomy is more common. Yet higher education is being asked to teach students how to work with people who have complementary skills and who are committed to a common purpose. More opportunities to practice teaming skills will be required. Perhaps the greatest dilemma stems from the fact that team skills are weak or non-existent among existing faculty, administrators, and staff. Without team skills themselves, or instruction in those skills, how can they teach them to others?

INTERPERSONAL SKILLS

Knowing how to work with others is critical—personally as well as professionally. The importance of interpersonal skills is a vital element in relating and interacting with clients and customers, and clearly represents an important issue for most organizations (Harvey and Knight 1996). In a sense, interpersonal skills are the "glue" that holds all the other attributes together. Good interpersonal skills are valuable because they

- facilitate communication of ideas with others at all levels, within and outside the organization;
- are necessary to influence people and thereby effect action; and
- facilitate appropriate interaction with clients or customers.

Do colleges and universities provide students with opportunities to develop work-related interpersonal skills such as feedback, encouragement, delegation, or recognition? These interpersonal skills form a set of core competencies for managers, not just workers. Managers can have a significant impact (positive or negative) on employees depending on whether they are positive, negative, attentive, or reclusive. Particularly at the management level, the importance of interpersonal skills is much deeper than "getting along." It is also about getting work done. In many respects, delegation is an interpersonal skill. At its best, delegation allows others to use and develop their skills and knowledge more completely. To enable someone to do a job for you, they must know what you want, have the authority to achieve it, and know how to do it. Delegation is rarely successful without both communication and interpersonal skills.

SOLVING PROBLEMS AND MAKING DECISIONS

Irrespective of career changes, the common denominators of the workplace are becoming problem solving and decision making. They are transferable skills that can be developed throughout a student's educational career. For example, if problem solving were taught within the curriculum, would students become familiar with the six steps in the problem-solving cycle? Although not always completed in the same order, at some point solving a problem typically requires passing through all six steps.

1. **Problem recognition.** To solve a problem, one must first recognize that there is a problem.
2. **Problem definition.** Once a problem is recognized, it needs to be correctly defined. Time and effort can be wasted trying to solve problems that do not exist. Typically, the more time spent defining the problem, the less time it takes to solve. (In studies of brighter versus less-bright problem solvers, brighter problem solvers spent relatively more time—up front—figuring out what to do and less time doing it. Less bright problem solvers spend less time figuring out what to do and more time doing it because they have not really defined the problem.)
3. **Formulating a strategy for problem solving.** Once a problem is defined, the individual or group needs to devise a strategy for solving it. Successful problem solvers invest significant resources devising strategies. They also focus on long-range rather than bottom-line strategies and are more willing to delay gratification. (Research has found that individuals who are better able to delay gratification as children demonstrate higher scores on tests of cognitive abilities as adolescents.)

4. **Representing information.** How information is represented when solving problems has a substantial effect on both what the ultimate solution is and its resolution.

5. **Allocating resources.** In solving a problem, we need to decide what resources to allocate to the problem. Smart people allocate time in an effective manner, spending just as long as a task is worth. They also reallocate resources if they are not getting the results they want.

6. **Monitoring and evaluation.** Monitoring means keeping track of progress during the process of problem solving; evaluation is our judgment of the quality of our problem-solving process as well as the solution reached. These are the final, analytical steps in problem solving (Sternberg 1996).

Unfortunately, many problems are poorly defined, especially by those without any training in problem solving. Problems with clear paths to solutions are called *well-structured problems* (e.g., "How do you find the area of a parallelogram?"). Problems without clear solution paths are termed *ill-structured problems* (e.g., "How do you succeed in a career of your choice?"). Strategies that work in solving well-structured problems often do not work well—or at all—for ill-structured problems (Sternberg 1996).

Education tends to emphasize well-structured problems—those with a clear, correct solution. Well-structured problems can often be solved by algorithms, which are formulas that, if followed, guarantee an accurate solution. Algorithms generally involve successive, somewhat mechanical iterations of a particular strategy until the correct solution is reached. Ill-structured problems are not so readily solved. They require entirely different strategies that fall into the realm of heuristics—intuitive, speculative strategies that sometimes work and other times don't.

The heuristic approach to problem solving is, by definition, a process that leads a person to find a solution by himself or herself. The difference between the heuristic and the algorithmic approaches can be seen in the way science is taught in our classrooms and the way it is practiced in a research lab. In an undergraduate science lab, students are presented with a problem, then follow a series of prescribed, algorithmic steps to find the solution. In a research lab, scientists do not work on problems that can be readily solved by formulas. Instead, they tackle problems whose solutions are not yet known and must be found by their own work, i.e., heuristically (Sternberg 1996).

Are our faculty trained in problem-solving approaches? When students are presented with problems, do those problems represent situations that must be solved with a mix of algorithmic approaches and heuristic approaches? Can our faculty help students improve their problem-solving processes as well as understand the final answers?

Along with problem solving comes decision making. The days of a parent-child relationship between management and employees are gone from business. In our flattened organizations we expect employees to make decisions. Speed of execution is critical to us, thus we expect decisions to be framed and made efficiently. It is no longer assumed that only the manager will make the decision or, conversely, that consensus is required. It is becoming standard practice to ask who really needs to be involved in the decision-making process and how. Consensus is sought only when there is a stated purpose for needing everyone to agree. When differences of opinion arise, criteria for making the decision are discussed and a variety of possible solutions are invented before deciding which is best. Does higher education teach students the decision-making process? Are students allowed to practice these skills on complex, real-world problems? Do faculty understand how decisions are made in business and industry? Are faculty skilled in this process themselves (Verville 1996)?

CREATIVITY

In today's economy, only organizations that find ways to trap the creativity of their employees are likely to survive (Bennis and Biederman 1996). Creativity involves making new and unusual connections by bringing together seemingly unrelated ideas, objects, or events in a way that leads to a new conception (Carlsen 1991). Creative ideas are, by definition, both novel and valuable.

According to Sternberg (1996), part of creativity is the ability to go beyond the given to generate novel and interesting ideas. Often, someone who is creative is a particularly good synthetic thinker, seeing connections (syntheses) other people do not see. The second aspect of creativity is analytical intelligence, the ability to analyze and evaluate ideas, solve problems, and make decisions. All people—even the most creative among us—have better and worse ideas. Creative people must have the ability to analyze their own ideas and evaluate their merit. The third aspect of creativity, practical intelligence, is the ability to translate theory into practice and more abstract ideas into practical accomplishments.

Developing creativity is the subject of books, workshops, even complete courses. Among the most important requirements for developing creativity is the need for a creative role model. Other characteristics associated with creativity are the ability to question assumptions, to make mistakes (and learn from them), to take sensible risks, and to define and redefine problems, as well as the ability to tolerate ambiguity.

How does higher education help students develop their creativity? Are students provided with opportunities to do creative, synthetic work? Are they provided with practice in putting their creative ideas into practice? Could they analyze a customer situation, develop financing, and market a new product?

LEADERSHIP

Leadership is crucial to organizations in a state of flux. By definition, leaders lead change. Leadership is a prerequisite to the flexible organization.

When life is orderly, tasks are predictable, and most things are going well, people neither want nor need much leadership. People tend to be content with what already exists. Change involves a gentle tweaking of the existing system in order to slowly improve it (Bardwick 1996). However, the type of leadership required in times of intense change differs from that needed when change is incremental.

Focus is one component that alters. In the past many leaders

> succeeded by focusing on the needs of their own organization and by being the best advocate for the interests of their own group. They could attract resources to their institution and then defend its borders, drawing distinctions between insiders and outsiders, "us" and "them," and keeping outsiders at arm's length. Leaders of the future can no longer afford to maintain insularity. It is simply not an option in an increasingly borderless world of boundariless organizations driven by "customer power." The fact is that people can increasingly bypass local monopolies or protected local suppliers and shop the world for the best goods and services. In short, leaders of the past often erected walls. Now they must destroy those walls and replace them with bridges. (Kanter 1996, 90–91)

Kanter (1996) applies the term *cosmopolitans* to leaders who are comfortable operating across boundaries and who can forge links between organizations. These leaders encourage people from diverse functions, disciplines, and organizations to work toward goals that improve an entire industry, community, country, or world, expanding the pie for everyone, rather than pitting group against group. They become *cosmopolitans* who have the vision, skills, and resources to form networks that extend beyond their home bases and to bring benefits to their own groups by partnering with others.

"Cosmopolitan leaders of the future must be *integrators* who can look beyond obvious differences among organizations, sectors, disciplines, functions, or cultures. They must be *diplomats* who can resolve conflicts between the different ways that organizations operate and who can influence people to work together. They must be *cross-fertilizers* who can bring the best from one place to another. And they must be deep thinkers who are smart enough to see new possibilities and conceptualize them" (Kanter 1996, 97).

What opportunities does higher education provide for students to develop leadership skills? If not in courses, then in extracurricular activities? Do faculty and administrators serve as role models of effective leaders? Would the operative definition of leadership displayed in your institution be insular or ecumenical? How are students encouraged to develop integration skills, conflict resolution skills, and other skills that help build bridges rather than erect walls?

PROJECT MANAGEMENT

The increasing complexity of the workplace has led to a greater need for project management skills. Individuals can use project management skills to manage their own work as well as to manage complex projects. Project management is the set of methods, principles, tools, and techniques for the effective management of work; it gives one person responsibility for ensuring the success of a project (Bivins 1998).

The steps involved in project management can be equally as well applied to complex problems as to completing a term paper. Among the stages of project management are:

- defining the project
- determining how one will solve the problem—what one needs to do and how to do it
- separating the work into discrete activities
- allocating the tasks to different people, ordering the tasks in a logical sequence
- developing a realistic estimate of the time involved in doing discrete tasks and the time required to reach milestones
- maintaining communication
- resolving conflicts

In many respects, project management is a skill that incorporates many of the attributes described earlier: interpersonal skills, communication, problem solving, etc. Reviewing a list of the most common reasons that projects fail highlights practical applications of many of these skills:

- losing sight of or lack of clear objectives
- lack of approval and commitment in the project initiation phase
- no clear conflict resolution procedure
- inappropriate members on the project team who can be neither trained nor transferred
- poor estimating skills for time or financial commitment
- lack of relevant experience or technical skills on the project team

- change in the thrust or direction of the project as personnel change
- lack of "political" support
- poor procedures for making changes
- communication problems (IBM 1993)

Does higher education provide students with the opportunities to develop project management skills? Are complex problems integrated into the curriculum? Are faculty trained in project management so they can pass the skills along to students?

Organizing a project is not enough. Getting it done is what ultimately counts. Execution is a critical skill in business, one that is too often lacking. Executing commitments—following through—is a requirement. However, in a smaller workforce faced with more diverse tasks, understanding what is being asked and the resources needed for execution is an increasingly important requirement. It goes beyond getting asked to do something, agreeing to do it, and working on the task. The final—often forgotten—phase is testing to see if the task has been fulfilled to the satisfaction of the requester. Do students learn how to make commitments only after they are clear about what is being asked for and why? Do they know how to clarify expectations? Do they learn to say no when they believe they cannot live up to what is being asked? When they say yes do they take time to review exactly what they are agreeing to do? Do they know how to ensure they have the resources to execute the commitment? Although one would not expect all students to enroll in a commitment management course, are these skills incorporated into the curriculum (Verville 1996)?

CONTINUOUS LEARNING

The volume of new information is increasing at such a rapid pace that the class of 2000 will be exposed to more new data in a year than their grandparents encountered in a lifetime. The evidence of the information explosion is all around us.

- Ten thousand scientific articles are published every day (Forman 1995).
- As of May 1996, there were more than 33 million articles and Web pages. It would take over five years to read just the new listings added each month (Van Alstyne 1996).
- Beginning in 1907, the Chemical Abstracts Society took 31 years to accumulate its first million abstracts; the next million took 18 years, and the most recent took 1.75. More articles have been published on chemistry in the last two years than in all of recorded history before 1900 (Noam 1995).

- The number of scientific and technical journals in print has literally doubled every 15 years in the twentieth century; the number is approaching 800,000 titles (Prusak 1997a).

With such rapid growth in the amount of information, it is almost axiomatic that the half-life of many college and university degrees will get shorter every year. It is estimated that the shelf life of a technical degree today is only five years. Although many of the critical skills required in the high-performance workplace have not changed, the pace of knowledge advancement requires constant updating (Verville 1995).

"Upskilling" is a focus on individual learning and the continuous enhancement of a person's skills and competencies. In the future, people will take more responsibility for their own careers. Individuals will need to develop the ability to assess their strengths and weaknesses, anticipate where their niches will be, and develop training/education programs to prepare for the next position. The days of stable employment, regular cost of living increases and/ or promotions are gone. To stay even or get ahead, employees will need to understand more than their own jobs—they will need to understand the "big picture," continuously improve their skills, and anticipate several career changes over a lifetime.

More and more, employees are recognizing that the ability to learn and continuously improve one's skills is the best source of job security. According to the Society for Training and Development, by 2000, 75 percent of the current workforce will need to be retrained just to keep up. Those companies that provide educational opportunities—either in-house or by subsidizing external education—are more desirable to employees. Part of the reason is that employees are looking for portable skills. It is accepted that people will work for four to five companies in their lifetimes. This causes employees to focus more on employment security rather than on job security. They want the skills that ensure they will always be employable, even if a given job is eliminated.

Building and applying competencies is necessary in a fast-paced, ever-changing business environment. The competencies of people are important assets to business—on a par with products or services. Although few would argue that lifelong learning is a requirement, how is this attitude fostered in the curriculum?

PRACTICAL EXPERIENCE

When asked what colleges and universities could do to better prepare students for the world of work, one of the most commonly mentioned suggestions is for students to gain practical experience, oftentimes through internships. Internships are seen as a way in which students can begin to apply what they have learned in class as well as develop an awareness of the corporate culture. The skill development, maturity, self-confidence, and competitiveness of students who have participated in internships is generally superior to those who have not had the opportunity.

Practical experience, whether from internships or other work-related opportunities, gives students a taste of a career and better allows them to decide what to do after graduation. Recent graduates say internships were valuable for the insights they provided into the work culture but that they also allowed them to become productive sooner on the job. Specific skills that are often cited as helpful are teamwork, time management, prioritization, and management skills (Harvey et al. 1997).

Students who have had internships often do better on interviews. How do you suspect a student who has had an internship might respond to these questions? What about one without an internship experience?

- Tell me about the most complex technical problem you have had to deal with. What made this a difficult or complicated problem? What knowledge or techniques did you use to deal with the problem? Did someone else assist you? What happened? How did it all turn out?
- Tell me about a time when you were a member of a work group or a team where some of the members were not doing their part and this was slowing down the group's progress. How did you feel about this situation? What happened? What do you think should have been done about this? How would you have handled the situation?
- Customers can often have very high expectations and may be challenging to work with. Tell me about a specific experience in which you had to deal with an angry customer. What made this a particularly difficult situation? How did you feel toward the customer during the interaction? What strategies did you use to handle the situation?

At many institutions, the preparation for these types of interview questions would be relegated to the placement office. Although career development and placement offices can assist students with developing resumes and presenting themselves well, there is little they can do to provide students with the kinds of skills these types of interview questions attempt to determine. Colleges and universities should ask themselves how often their students have the opportunity to work as teams on complex problems. What exposure have they had to customer situations? Could students identify or describe problem-solving strategies? Conflict resolution strategies? Motivational approaches?

Many in business and industry would declare today's graduates to be technically competent. However, few would agree that students acquire the problem-solving, interpersonal, or communication skills required for the job. This has led employers to develop a strong bias towards students who have had internship or cooperative experience. It is through real-world exposure that many of these skills are developed.

CONCLUSION

Business is changing. As business changes, what it needs from employees will shift. Most of all, business needs people who will enter the workplace ready to make a solid contribution but who will also be effective in the future. Leaders will be required who can anticipate and lead change. Graduates of higher education will need to be flexible, adaptable, and in possession of a mix of broad education and specific skills. Communication, interpersonal skills, problem solving, decision making, and teamwork are the competencies that will allow employees to grow and adapt as the world of work continues to change.

QUESTIONS TO ASK

- How often do faculty or administrators engage in discussions of what business needs from higher education?
- Are faculty aware of strategies that can be used to develop creative intelligence? Practical intelligence?
- Are students taught a variety of problem-solving strategies including algorithmic and heuristic ones?
- Are students provided with opportunities to develop skills such as negotiation or diplomacy?
- Are faculty effective team members instead of committee members?
- Are students exposed to teamwork — in theory and in practice? Are they prepared to work in a team environment?
- Do the grading systems of individual courses and of the institution reflect group collaboration and cooperation or simply individual competition?
- Is project management a skill to which students are introduced?
- What is higher education doing to make its students aware of the trend of upskilling and assuming responsibility for developing their own competencies?
- What kinds of interpersonal skills will be required in a diverse, global, team-based environment?
- How is the attitude of lifelong learning fostered by higher education?
- Are students internalizing a process where they ask themselves questions such as: What are my competencies? What value have I created through applying these competencies? What skills/capabilities do I need to gain or deepen? What new competencies do I need? What specific steps will I take to do this?

- What roles do curricula and student services play in helping students build and apply their competencies?
- How does your institution develop creativity in students?
- Are you providing your students the opportunity to work as a part of a team over a distance? In a cross-cultural setting?
- Is technology a competency your students can demonstrate upon graduation? Is it a competency your faculty possess? Your graduate students?

CHAPTER 7

The Learning Environment

usiness leaders are convinced that students are not prepared to enter
into today's fast-moving global business environment. Recently employed alumni complain about poor preparation in a number of areas,
the lack of practical, hands-on business experience among faculty, and deficiencies in career guidance and counseling. Ironically, academic leaders do
not see themselves as key agents in curricular change, especially in light of
sometimes hostile faculty (ACE 1997).

What business needs from higher education is a more responsive, learner-
centered environment. Flexibility and adaptability of content as well as
flexibility and adaptability of delivery will be critical. Learners are becoming
more diverse in terms of gender, ethnicity, age, and educational goals. A
system designed to serve 18–22-year-olds in a residential setting is inadequate
for the emerging cadre of lifelong learners. Faculty who are subject-matter
specialists but who have little contact with the "real world" may be unable to
bridge theory to application well enough for those learners who are seeking an
edge in a competitive job market.

We do not advocate an education system driven solely by a business
agenda. Corporate leaders do not view themselves as curriculum experts, nor
do they seek to supplant the faculty. Yet, they can—and should—comment on
the quality of their new hires. Society needs an educational environment that
will develop successful intelligence, moving beyond just analytical intelligence
to include creativity and practicality. We know a great deal about learners and

learning. The challenge will be to more thoroughly integrate what we know into the existing education system.

FEATURES OF A NEW EDUCATIONAL MODEL

How would one design an educational system if one could begin from scratch? If we had not inherited the existing physical infrastructure, organizational hierarchy, traditions, and biases, the educational model chosen would likely be quite different from the one we have today. Characteristics would include being learning centered, flexible, adaptable, and responsive as well as giving a high priority to advisement. Even though we cannot design an educational system, *de novo*, we can identify the desirable characteristics that should be integrated into our existing structures.

Learning Centered

The historic model for higher education, perhaps tracing back 2,500 years, is for information to be collected in a library, a monastery, or on a campus. Scholars clustered around the information, and around each other. Students came to the scholars. The focal point was access to the information. However, IT is fundamentally changing this model. Information is almost instantly available from any location, at any time of day. Scholars operate in electronic communities. The focal point can shift to the learner. "Today's production and distribution of information are undermining the traditional flow of information and with it the university structure. . . . In the past, people came to the information, which was stored at the university. In the future, the information will come to the people, wherever they are" (Noam 1995, 247, 249).

Focus on the learner

Historically, undergraduate education has operated on the premise that the student spends four years living on a campus, insulated from home, work, and social environments outside the campus. Consequently, it is a campus-centric system that is both place-constrained (the campus or the classroom) and time-constrained (delivered according to an academic calendar and a specific course schedule that is controlled by the provider). The campus-centric model assumes that students will choose from a campus-established set of courses and curricula. Control over the content is in the hands of the provider—the faculty or the institution. Administrative functions such as admissions, financial aid, and registration are designed for the convenience of the institution with less regard for the needs of the consumer.

At least rhetorically, many colleges and universities are changing the framework of their learning and student service environments. Most of our institutions have inherited a model where a particular office or function behaves as if it is at the center of the student's universe; students must move from place to place or from person to person. The emerging model places the student at the center, with more flexible access to people and information.

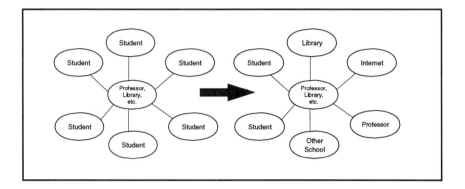

Consumer orientation

Why are colleges and universities changing from an institution-centered to a learning-centered environment? Because it confers a competitive advantage. It is consumer-oriented. It is user-friendly. Although there are any number of philosophical answers to the question, the bottom line is that students are behaving as increasingly savvy consumers. They are taking their "business" to institutions that are more learning centered.

One indication of the rising power of learners is the trend for students to learn independent of time and place. The assumption that higher education takes place in the classroom or on the campus must change as learning is shifted to the workplace, the home, the library, or even the network. Communications technologies enable a shift toward asynchronous (at different times) rather than synchronous (at the same time) learning experiences, which makes learning available seven days a week, 24 hours a day. Increasingly learners use networks to interact with peers, instructors, and external experts, as well as information resources; they do it when it is convenient for them, not just during scheduled class times (Twigg and Oblinger 1997).

Consider student services as another example in which the learning-centered philosophy is becoming increasingly important. In the traditional student services model, each office focuses on a specific area of responsibility. The admissions office focuses on recruiting and enrolling applicants, the office of financial aid concerns itself with providing financial assistance to students, and so on. This model does not meet the needs of students because it artificially segregates the services students require. It also presents challenges for administrators as they try to be more service oriented. It is difficult to provide a holistic or service-oriented environment for the student when major processes are segregated, systems are not integrated, communication is limited, and administrative and academic functions are not linked (Beede and Burnett 1998).

Any individual who has spent time on a campus is familiar with the phenomenon of the student being passed from office to office, waiting in line each time, and growing more and more frustrated as a seemingly simple task takes a great deal of time and energy. Today's students/consumers have grown up in a society where superior service delivery and the use of technology is the norm. In addition, as the non-traditional student population grows they will demand services—not just courses—that are time- and location-independent. With only a few exceptions, today's student services are neither student centered nor compatible with the needs of the lifelong learner.

Everyone learns

Being learning centered implies that campuses believe in the value of ongoing learning for everyone. To create a sophisticated and continually improving workforce, we need to create and nurture learning organizations. "How institutions of higher education engage their workforces in learning activities is one of our sadder ironies. Colleges and universities are, of course, learning organizations by definition. . . . If we are to develop sophisticated problem solvers in our organizations, we will need to increase our commitments to the formal training agenda. In addition, we will need to discover, uncover, empower and replicate that complex informal system of successful mentorships, peer networks, informal collaborations and grapevines that exist already in the organization" (Ernst et al. 1996, 15–16).

Becoming a learning organization mirrors the individual's commitment to learning. For singular workers, brains, know-how, broad skills, and the willingness to learn throughout life have become the essential tools for building a career (ACE 1997). Job skills are more important than a job alone. In the university of the twenty-first century, employees should recognize that their jobs and security will depend more on their own competence and work skills than on the hierarchy. Assessing skills, finding good teachers, and making time for self-improvement will become part of the college and university culture. The goal will be to ensure that employees have skills that are valuable and transferable.

Responsibility

Being learning centered implies new responsibilities for students as well as for the institution. One is that students must work. When the student is defined as the worker, learning occurs not when teachers lecture or demonstrate, but when students are engaged in the learning process. It takes two to tango: a teacher and a student, or a textbook and a students or a computer and a student, or a field experience and a student. The only constant is the student—the involved and interested student. The fact is, learning is hard work, plain and simple. Satisfying, rewarding, to be sure, but hard work nonetheless. It need not be disagreeable work, but it will always require diligence, application, effort, and attentiveness (Gerstner et al. 1994).

The new learning environments and skills that will be required of students are likely to demand additional effort even though IT can make learning more motivating, engaging, and enjoyable. In a learning-centered environment students will be responsible and accountable for many activities ranging from updating their mailing addresses to seeking external experts for course projects. Institutions can make the processes simpler, but they are not obligated to assume the *in loco parentis* burden. For all involved, becoming learning centered will require some adjustment.

In a more collaborative and participatory educational environment students must also become responsible for being mentors and tutors. The opportunity to help another person learn is one of life's great pleasures, and students should know the feeling early. Students can tutor each other or work with younger children. Indeed, younger children can often tutor older children , or even tutor adults, as any parent who has struggled with a recalcitrant VCR knows. Frequently the children are the real technology experts, from confronting complicated computer programming to running and understanding routine programs (Gerstner et al. 1994).

Flexible and Adaptable

Nearly two centuries ago, our nation began its shift from an agricultural to an industrial economy. The needs of students and society shifted radically. The institutions that emerged were those that responded to these new needs—the land-grant colleges and universities. "In the post–World War II era, higher education again faced a period of radical change as vast numbers of returning GIs filled our universities and a college education became a common aspiration for all levels of our society. Today, we face a third era of change as we shift from a national to a global economic system and as the driving force of economic wealth increasingly becomes the production of knowledge itself instead of the production of things. The speed of change, for the first time, has become the defining theme of our age" (Duderstadt 1996, 6).

Much of what we currently offer students is constrained by the existing infrastructure, the experience base of the faculty, and the funding mechanisms of our institutions. Ideally, students would be able to learn in a time- and location-independent fashion. The learning environment would adapt (within reason) to their pace. As every teacher knows, not all students can progress at the same rate. Further confounding the learning and developmental speed of each learner is the individual's ability to focus on instruction. Frequently job or family requirements will impact the pace at which a student can proceed. If our institutions are truly learning centered, they will accommodate learner needs for varied points of entry and exit. Students enter learning situations with variable preparation for the subject. Not all students seek the same level of mastery. With appropriate assessment and modularization of the content and delivery, much of the learning environment can be customized. We need new models for higher education that are more flexible and adaptable to respond to the increasing pace of change in business and society.

Redefining learning

Colleges and universities must continue to redefine learning, particularly where the operative definition of learning has been restricted to teaching. There is ample evidence that learning is not always dependent on teaching. We also know that learning is a social process and interactivity is closely linked to the learning achieved. Cognition, learning models, and individual learning styles must be taken into account, not ignored.

In part, we need to redefine learning because learners and their needs have changed. The students of higher education are becoming more heterogeneous. Their time is valuable. Their needs are for education, skills, and attitudes. To meet these needs, a new type of learning environment will be required where

- programs of study are more individualized, with educational planning done more by competency than by discipline or job;
- instruction is provided in modules (not just in courses) that will allow learners to review and refresh their knowledge as well as complete traditional courses;
- testing is embedded and continuous rather than being an explicit event;
- instruction is multi-sensory, accommodating various learning styles; and
- learners initiate educational activities themselves.

Looking a few years into the future, "it will become abnormal to require a student to be in the same room with a professor 45 times during a semester. Learning will occur whenever students can connect to the World Wide Web. Students will be able to move easily among educational institutions, perhaps simultaneously enrolling at several real and/or virtual universities, or studying one subject at the high school level and other subjects with college professors" (Langenberg 1997, A64).

Teaching and learning can and should be redesigned. The tools and techniques currently available allow us to fundamentally rethink and redesign education to improve performance, cost, quality, service, and responsiveness. Massy (1997) presents a scenario based on the teaching of microeconomics that illustrates what might be possible if reengineering were applied to instruction.

Reengineering applied to instruction

The traditional method of teaching microeconomics usually involves a combination of lecture and discussion sessions on a fixed schedule, supplemented with reading and homework assignments. The reengineered method might employ a combination of lectures, interactive studio sessions using simulations and multimedia packages, and small-group discussions with faculty about meaning and relevance—discussions rich in personal interaction and mentoring as well as knowledge transmission—all on a flexible schedule geared to student needs.

Massy describes how a hypothetical reengineered course might appear to students as they learn microeconomics theory and its practical applications, and to faculty as they carry out their teaching duties. The scenario illustrates the kinds of qualitative benefits—for students and for faculty—that can be achieved through reengineering.

> "What is microeconomics and what is it good for?" These natural questions are addressed in a series of three or four lectures at the beginning of the learning process. The department recruits its most charismatic lecturer for this assignment and the professor gives her all in preparing and delivering the material. Being chosen for this assignment becomes an important element of recognition by one's colleagues. Convening in a large group provides a sense of excitement, which the professor reinforces by using state-of-the-art multimedia to illustrate and punctuate important points—the students will remember these sessions many years later when much of the detail that comes later will have faded.

> Next the student embarks on a series of interactive studio and individual exercises using simulation and multimedia applications (supplemented with the familiar textbook) to develop competence in the course's first content module. The courseware's interactive character produces real-time diagnostics about student progress and difficulties as a byproduct of the learning process itself—diagnostics that can be used to design mitigations or control entry to the next learning stage. From the department's standpoint, the fact that much of the intellectual content is built into the materials enables more independent student work and more flexibility in staffing. For example, much of the work needed to bring students to proficiency with the courseware is handled by graduate students or support staff without any loss of effectiveness.

Once students have mastered the codified knowledge specified for a course module they move into small-group discussions with faculty about the non-codified dimensions. "What does the theory say at its deepest level? What objections have been raised and are there competing world-views? How can these concepts help in one's career and life generally?" Because students move into the small-group sessions only after they have demonstrated a requisite degree of understanding, the time with the professor is not dominated by elemental questions. These sessions take better advantage of the faculty's unique skills than restating codified wisdom in class after class.

Students advance to the subsequent course unit when they have completed the cycle for a given module. This may be gated on an individual basis, as when a student begins the next phase of technology-based independent work, or control may be through completion of the discussion sessions. Either way, student progress will not be bound to a fixed syllabus determined by the average student's ability and motivation. Students needing more time will get it—and still pass the course providing they attain the requisite learning threshold in a reasonable period of time. Better students can move ahead quickly, thus enabling them to gain more education or, at their discretion, reduce the time and cost of attaining the degree.

The scenario also illustrates another benefit from reengineering: it relaxes traditional constraints on the economics of the educational process. For example, faculty labor is applied at the times and in the circumstances needed rather than in fixed quanta defined inflexibly as courses per semester ("teaching loads"). Technology substitutes for some of what has traditionally been viewed as faculty work, but faculty labor is redeployed to tasks that professors can do best. Support staff and graduate student time may be used to a greater extent than in some kinds of institutions currently, but it is concentrated in areas where faculty do not have a comparative advantage—not in places, like small-group discussion sections, where a professor's wisdom can confer important benefits. The basic economic message is that redesign breaks the widely perceived link between expenditure per student (or the student-faculty ratio) and educational quality. (Massy 1997, 201–2)

Business needs higher education to be more concerned with the outcomes of instruction. The demands raised by new communications technologies, changing student demographics, the rising costs of a residential experience, and the need for continuing education throughout a lifetime cannot be met without change to this centuries-old system. Relationships among learners, instructors, and information resources are shifting. The *modus operandi* of the campus should be changing, as well. The rapid proliferation of information and communications technologies is making it possible for the control of delivery to move out of the hands of traditional providers—higher education institutions and faculty—and into the hands of consumers.

EXPAND OPTIONS WITH TECHNOLOGY

One of the great values of technology is that it expands options. Hundreds of years ago, the lecture was designed as a substitute for direct access to scholarly information. When books were a rare commodity, the closest students came to the authentic information was the lecture. Today our options range from original archives to digital books to three-dimensional representations that move about the world at the speed of light. If one asks the question, "Why do we teach the way we do?" the answer is often that we didn't know there were other options. This no longer needs to be true. With what we know about cognition and communication, lecture is only one style among many. Today, educators are presented with an array of options.

Access to IT can enhance learning in several ways. When compared to traditional classes, student satisfaction with online courses is higher, grade point averages and other measures of student achievement are the same or better, a higher level of critical thinking and problem solving is reported, and there is often more discussion among students and instructors in a course. Instructors are able to track the progress of their students in a detailed way and have a better understanding of what students are or are not learning. Computer networking provides a more "authentic" learning environment in the sense that students can easily communicate with other educational professionals outside of the class or group if they desire (Kearsley et al. 1995).

The Value of Technology

Getting connected

Technology enables the transmission of information. But fundamentally, the critical process is people interacting with other people. Technology brings value to education because it allows people to "get connected" to information, to other students, to instructors, and to external experts. These connections allow learners and teachers the opportunity to expand beyond what is locally available and access new ideas, perspectives, cultures, and information.

Connections to vast digital repositories of original information are increasingly available. Collections from museums, libraries, and archives can be browsed, queried, and studied, worldwide, for the first time. This access to the original source material brings students closer to the level of scholarship that faculty experience. It is through working with authentic material, coupled with learning the "way of thinking" of a particular scholarly community, that students enhance their learning.

Getting connected allows faculty and students to use computer-mediated communication to enhance teaching and learning. It can help break down time and location barriers, allow for interpersonal distance, enable students to access information in a self-paced exploratory fashion, reinforce learning, and allow for and encourage self-directed learning. A large range of activities— e-mail, use of listservs, computer conferencing, the use of databases, collaborative projects, real-time chat and teacher-student, teacher-teacher, and student-student interactions are among the options available for those who get connected (Ellsworth 1994).

In the workplace, using electronic resources to find information and solve problems is a necessity. Developing these skills while in college is an advantage. Faculty and library personnel can help students learn to navigate digital resources as well as assess the quality and reliability of sources.

Participation and interaction

Studies have shown that when collaboration takes place through the computer, student participation is enhanced rather than inhibited (Harasim et al. 1995). There are several reasons for this:

- students participate at a time and place that is convenient to them
- participants have time to compose questions, comments, or answers before typing them
- even after input is typed, it can be studied and revised before being submitted
- student comments are not interrupted by others
- inhibiting factors, such as shyness or lack of confidence in oral skills, are minimized
- the discussion cannot be dominated by any single individual

Technology can allow students to easily interact with their classmates, regardless of whether they may be dispersed around the country or across the world. Although the face-to-face method may be the most efficient form of communication, such meetings do not occur very often (or at all when classmates span the globe). Networked communication allows students to communicate 24 hours a day, seven days a week, asynchronously. The result is that, averaged over several days, more frequent and effective interaction with asynchronous communication can be much higher than face-to-face communication (Mayadas 1997).

Many faculty express concern that an online environment is impersonal. The student viewpoint is often quite different. Students do not necessarily require the kind of socializing that goes on in many classrooms. Teaching online can and does foster a sense of closeness between student and instructor (Jaeger 1991).

More equitable access

Delivery of education through a collaborative, computer-mediated environment alters the relationships among the instructor, the students, and the course content. The many-to-many, asynchronous nature of the medium "democratizes" access and encourages student input (Harasim 1991). In fact, research is showing that students often find technology both liberating and more personal than traditional instruction.

In research on asynchronous learning environments, one consistent finding is that students feel they have more access to the professor than they did in traditional lecture courses. In addition, they feel they have more interaction with other students. Studies reveal the positive aspects of asynchronous learning.

- Online courses are distinguished by active peer-to-peer discussion and exchange.
- Messaging is fairly evenly distributed among students. Online interaction displays fewer extremes, such as dominant input by a few individuals and little or no participation by anyone else in class.
- There are increased opportunities for access offered by the asynchronous, place-independent environment.
- Asynchronicity provides learners with time to formulate ideas and contribute responses. Students report that asynchronicity enables them to participate more actively and effectively.
- Group interaction is motivating to students and exposes them to a diverse range of perspectives. Students read input from all other students, rather than the ideas of only the instructor and a few students (Harasim 1993).

Interaction through networks helps break down communication barriers and inhibitions that often stifle the open exchange of ideas in traditional classrooms (Eisenberg and Ely 1993).

Active learning

As a general principle of good practice, learning must be active. "Learning is not a spectator sport. Students do not learn much just sitting in classes listening to teachers, memorizing prepackaged assignments, and spitting out answers. They must talk about what they are learning, write reflectively about it, relate it to past experiences and apply it to their daily lives. They must make what they learn part of themselves" (Chickering and Ehrmann 1996, 4).

Among the range of technologies that encourage active learning is apprentice-like learning. Although traditionally supported by libraries, laboratories, and art studios, newer technologies can now enrich and expand these opportunities. Technology can be used to support apprentice-like activities. In fields that require the use of technology as a tool, the Internet or World Wide Web can be used to gather information. Computer simulations can illustrate and animate difficult concepts. They can also help students gain insight (Chickering and Ehrmann 1996).

Supercomputers are being used to visually model complex proteins and enzymes and watch them interact in human-like environments. Architects are using computer imaging to tour buildings before they exist. They can light a virtual building to see it at night, shine the sun on it to check reflections and shadows, or simulate an earthquake or fire. Ecologists are translating the millions of atmospheric and oceanic samples gathered around the globe into animated pictures to monitor ocean pollution, the spread of crop disease, and changes in ozone levels (Broad 1992).

Graduates of programs that provide hands-on experience with IT and the tools of the profession are finding that they have a competitive edge in the job market. In addition, students who practice the skills and concepts they are taught in the classroom are more likely to be able to remember and use them later in life.

Improves motivation

Network use is highly motivational for both students and instructors. Many faculty who use networks describe a new energy and enthusiasm often missing in more conventional classrooms. This results from the ability to share ideas, concerns, and solutions with peers—no matter where they are—as easily as if they were in the next room. Instructional formats, based on heavy interaction with technology and team-based collaboration, release important reserves of student motivation that tend to be stifled under traditional lecture-based delivery. This in turn has the potential to yield greater "learner productivity" (D. Jones 1996).

Another element that is different for students with online opportunities is the chance to see the work of others and to compare their ideas with those of their classmates. Students learn not only from their own work but from everyone else. By its very nature, this kind of online environment encourages collaboration and group interaction (Kearsley et al. 1995). Students also appear to be more motivated when they realize their work will be viewed by their peers.

Accelerates instructional "throughput"

The use of IT in education presents the opportunity to make learning more efficient by cutting both the time and the volume of instructional activity needed for students to earn credentials. One reason this opportunity exists is that flexible self-paced formats allow students to test-out of content. Second, more coherent and streamlined curricular designs can allow students to complete needed coursework earlier than they might have done otherwise. Third, the quality of "time-independence" allows students to circumvent typically encountered course-availability blockages in high-demand courses. And fourth, more coherent course sequences can significantly reduce the "rework" associated with students failing to effectively master prerequisite skills taught (or not taught) in earlier courses (D. Jones 1996).

Not for everyone

It would be incorrect to imply that there is a single "right" way to educate. Learning styles and preferences differ from one individual to another. Another set of unique variables is interjected by subject matter and course objectives. Not everyone adapts easily or well to a technology-enhanced environment. In one study, for example, student evaluations and homework responses indicated that 80–85 percent of the students strongly preferred networked delivery of the curriculum. They found it easier to stay engaged with the material since it was always available. However, 15–20 percent of the students resented the use of computers, largely based on either their fear of technology or their perception that the curriculum was "dehumanized" by the machines (Bothun 1996). Although technology works for many students, faculty, and subjects, it is not a panacea. It is the ability of technology to allow us to present more choices in learning methods, teach in new ways and with greater convenience, that is of value, not the technology in and of itself.

The strength of technology is its flexibility. Although it frees us from constraints such as time, place, and institution, few have taken advantage of these new freedoms. If higher education were more adaptable, would it better serve the needs of society, business, and learners?

Collaboration

Dissatisfaction with the efficiency of the lecture paradigm as well as the need for employees who are adept at collaboration and teamwork is leading many to advocate a collaborative educational model. Greater interaction—student-to-faculty, student-to-student, and student-to-information—is directly related to improved learning (Fletcher 1991). Collaboration is growing as an alternative to lectures.

In collaborative learning, the *modus operandi* is for students to work in teams, negotiate the process and the outcomes, actively share information and ideas, and solve problems. This form of learning is a more social method than the one-to-many lecture. It also more closely mirrors real life and the work world. A team approach, extensive communication, and interaction, with significantly enhanced self-direction, should be emphasized. Collaboration can be either synchronous or asynchronous, another reflection of the world external to education. It can occur in a classroom or across many locations and many time zones.

A major goal of collaborative learning is the active involvement of students in learning activities. For example, by using massive, open-ended data from the Internet rather than just selected facts memorized from the traditional lecture, students must find and process information similar to what they will encounter on the job or in life. Students who become responsible for their own learning and collaboration are more likely to acquire the lifelong learning skills required in today's workplace.

There are other benefits of collaboration beyond learning. For example, the process of creating, analyzing, and evaluating (higher level thinking skills in Bloom's Taxonomy), when done in collaboration with others, strengthens socialization skills, increases cross-cultural awareness and appreciation, and increases general interest, focus, and synthesis efforts (Ellsworth 1994). These are skills often cited as lacking in new employees.

Make Advising Useful

Academic advising may be the key to a successful educational experience. Selecting the most suitable major, choosing the right courses in an optimal sequence, finding job and internship experiences, and handling growth in personal and professional maturity are all associated with good advising. How well it is done—or not done—can have as significant an impact on students as how well they are prepared for the workplace.

Recently employed alumni frequently complain about low-quality academic and career guidance that has left them "lost and floundering" in a maze of curricular possibilities and career options; poor courses or teachers, both of which wasted their time; faculty who lacked hands-on experience; and the lack of courses directly related to the world of work (ACE 1997).

Academic advising is traditionally viewed as providing all students—from first semester to senior year—with academic information and related assistance with planning. Generally, the focus is on students' progress in fulfilling graduation requirements and on the quality of academic information students receive. The view is prescriptive. An alternative is developmental advising in which the major goals are:

- growth in the self-awareness of the relationship of education and life
- growth in the ability to identify realistic academic and career goals as well as a program to achieve them
- growth in the awareness of life as extending beyond the college years (Kramer 1996)

In a lifelong context, this would be a much more valuable form of advising than one that focuses almost exclusively on academic rules, regulations, and course equivalencies.

The selection of courses and the scheduling of classes are where the majority of advisors spend their time today. Technology can easily facilitate providing those services while the advisors/counselors might spend their time facilitating the exploration of life goals (values), the exploration of educational/career goals, identification of mentors and role models, and the selection of educational programs. It is through these value-added activities that the student will derive the greatest benefits. It is also where they most need the skills of a professional to assist them in their development and goal attainment (Beede and Burnett 1998).

Assessment and Certification

Without measurable goals and outcomes, neither higher education nor its stakeholders can measure progress towards those goals. There are several opportunities for assessment: assessment prior to entering a course, assessment at the end of the course, certification of competency, and certification of degree completion.

Although many students are tested prior to entering first-year math or beginning foreign language courses, assessment of skills or knowledge prior to entering a course is the exception rather than the rule. Such an omission sends the signal that higher education cares less about optimizing human potential and time than it does having students "punch their tickets" as they move through a factory model of education. It also implies little respect for a student's time. If the student can demonstrate he or she has mastered the content and concepts that the course was designed to cover, the efficient approach would be to allow that individual to move on to the next learning experience. Higher education seems to be wedded to a seat-time model that may have little relevance to a world based on skills and competencies.

As lifelong learning becomes more common there are more requests to certify knowledge, whether the learner was enrolled in a credit-bearing course or not. In fact, the Western Governors University is designing assessment mechanisms that allow for the measurement and assessment of knowledge and proficiencies no matter what their source.

There are at least three reasons why assessment is not more common: (1) the lack of clear definitions of the outcomes and competencies to be gained as a result of a course, (2) the lack of good assessment measures, and (3) the lack of any incentives for the institution to allow students to "test out" of courses. In a model where institutional funding is based on students enrolled in classes rather than students successfully moving ahead, there is no incentive for certifying mastery. As in any system, behavior follows rewards. If we really believe in the value of time and that our human capital is a resource, can higher education afford to perpetuate this model? Legislators and the public are increasingly frustrated with higher education. Accountability, assessment, and funding are often intertwined. A proactive stance on assessment is needed because "if we do not create our own framework of skills and measurements, then legislators, trustees, and others beyond our walls will not hesitate to impose theirs on us" (Diamond 1997).

Public and policy leaders are skeptical of higher education's assessment and certification process. Does course completion signify the learner has mastered certain skills or a scholarly way of thinking? Or does it signify fees paid and minimal attendance met? Although the business community says it believes the bachelor's degree should prepare students for long-term employment and career growth, not just entry job skills, most people have difficulty defining what a liberal arts education is (Hersh 1997).

Some predict that there is significant risk that the baccalaureate degree will be devalued or will disappear altogether. There are non-traditional providers who work with employers to define desirable skills and design educational modules to provide them. Many expect the marketplace value of these certificates, which validate the acquisition of specific skills, to increase. Certificates will signify exactly what abilities have been mastered by the certificate holders and what employers can expect of them.

"If higher education cannot defend the baccalaureate degree as certifying specific abilities, employers are increasingly likely to opt for the certainty of certificates that tell them exactly what curricula a student has mastered and exactly what knowledge base a student has. If we believe the baccalaureate degree has significant value, the challenge is ours to articulate that value and to provide mechanisms of accountability that will ensure that every degree awarded does certify what we contend" (Hooker 1997, 29).

CONCLUSION

For higher education to provide students with the education and competencies they will need in a twenty-first century workplace, new models of the learning environment will be needed. This environment will be characterized by being learning centered, flexible, adaptable, and collaborative. Information technology will be used to expand the options available to both faculty and students.

QUESTIONS TO ASK

- How should we define a student-centered environment that suits the needs of students?

- What changes will need to be made so that a learning-centered environment permeates the entire institution, not just the administrative offices?
- Are we building the IT infrastructure that will allow us to create a more flexible and adaptable learning environment?
- Are we changing our attitudes and structures to support the belief that learning is everyone's business and that there are appropriate roles for faculty, staff, students, parents, alumni, and others?
- Is student success defined more in terms of how well students solve problems, communicate ideas, present information, and learn how to learn rather than how well they memorize what their instructors say?
- How have we made the curriculum problem centered? Are students engaged in tasks related to the real world in which they must collect and assess information to solve problems?
- Are subjects integrated? Are students exposed to different perspectives? Does the curriculum help students relate one subject to another?
- Are students developing the ability to use and interpret multiple sources of information, ranging from traditional print materials, to the Internet, to dialog with experts?
- How will the financial and administrative structures of the institution need to change in order to encourage more creative and effective learning models?
- Does our curriculum meet students' needs? Employers' needs? How do we know?
- How often do students have structured opportunities for collaboration and group work? Are they provided with an introduction to the skills necessary to work as part of a team?
- What skills needed in the workplace are integrated into the curriculum? Information technology? Interpersonal communications?
- How are alumni and outside experts brought into the students' academic experience?
- How do faculty develop and maintain an understanding of what business wants and needs in employees? Can they help students understand "the corporate culture"?
- Is our advising almost exclusively focused on assistance in fulfilling graduation requirements? Is there a proactive process that provides developmental advising to students?
- Are assessment strategies being effectively used to optimize student time and effort? Can the institution measure its effectiveness at the course level? Departmental or institutional level?
- Can we define what having a degree from our institution certifies?

CHAPTER

The Early Years

There are approximately 100,000 schools in the United States with more than 51 million children attending. The U.S. Department of Education's National Center for Education Statistics expects that number to grow to almost 56 million by 2005. These children are our future, and the legacies we give them will determine the kind of world in which they will live. The most critical of those legacies is their education—what they know, what they can do, and how they can acquire and use new knowledge as adults.

Student performance in the United States continues to be disappointing, with reading achievement at 12th grade decreasing and 13 percent of all college students requiring at least one remedial course. Almost 400,000 students drop out annually; high school graduation rates are only 86 percent. National reading performance is, at best, disappointing: 25 percent of fourth graders and 37 percent of 12th graders fail to reach the basic reading level standard, while only 16 percent of 12th graders reach the proficient math level standard. International comparisons can be striking: 37 percent of German students take advanced placement (AP) exams, with 95 percent of those taking the exams passing. Only 7 percent of U.S. students take the AP exams and of those, only 66 percent pass (Verville 1997).

PRECOLLEGE PREPARATION

Evidence continues to accumulate that our schools are not preparing students to be effective citizens of our world. As education goes, so goes our economy, our society, our culture. The greatest challenge we now face as a nation is the need to overcome the inadequate education, and hence the inadequate skills, of our citizens. Americans as a whole are in serious danger of being unable to reason, analyze, compute, or even communicate effectively with one another. Less than 20 percent of fourth, eighth, and 12th graders in 1990 were able to pass competency tests for their grade level in mathematics, and results for 1991 were scarcely better (Johnstone 1994).

Businesses are beginning to acknowledge literacy as a long-denied problem. Nine of 10 *Fortune 1000* CEOs recognize illiteracy as a problem in the American workplace. Virtually all chief executives agree that workers' literacy levels affect productivity and profitability in general; 77 percent say that it has an effect on their own businesses. The U.S. Department of Labor estimates that illiteracy costs U.S. businesses about $225 billion a year in lost productivity. The costs stem from employee mistakes, injuries, absenteeism, tardiness, missed opportunities, and other problems associated with illiteracy (Reese 1996).

The problem is not limited to our young people. In recent tests fewer than 13 percent of adults could identify the main argument in a newspaper article, and only 14 percent could use a bus schedule or calculate percentages for a tip in a restaurant. Current estimates suggest that fully 25 percent of American adults are functionally illiterate. Even among higher level employees, skill levels can be shocking: the Department of Education estimates that more than 10 percent of all managerial, technical, and professional employees are "functional illiterates" (Johnstone 1994).

These deficiencies are translating into workforce problems. Companies reporting labor shortages are increasing. Nearly one-half of companies surveyed report skilled worker shortages, and one in 10 companies are reporting unskilled worker shortages.

| | Percentage of Companies Reporting | |
	Skilled Worker Shortages	Unskilled Worker Shortages
April 1995	30.1	4.1
April 1997	47.3	10.7

Source: National Association of Business (NAB). 1997d. Paper from Business Policy Council for Workforce Development, 21 May, 3.

EFFECTIVENESS OF K–12

Closely related to the issue of student preparedness for the twenty-first century workforce is the effectiveness of our public school system. In a society where education is linked to economic benefit and social stability, higher education can play a major role in helping to solve these problems. While many of the employees that American businesses hire are graduates of postsecondary institutions, even more are graduates of our K–12 system who never enter higher education. Business needs high school graduates. Many jobs do not require a college diploma but they do require well-educated individuals. Even though these students are not direct "products" of higher education, their teachers are. By better preparing and supporting teachers, higher education can improve the preparedness of high school graduates.

In our economic and social life we expect change, but in the public schools we have clung tenaciously to the ideas and techniques of earlier decades— even previous centuries. In many ways the public school classroom of today is indistinguishable from the classrooms of our parents and grandparents. A teacher stands in front of 20–30 children for seven hours per day, imparting a version of the knowledge contained in fraying textbooks and dogeared workbooks. A principal, with little authority, runs the school as part of a large, hierarchical system. Schools look like industrial plants from a vanished era. A time traveler from 1942—or perhaps even one from 1892—would easily recognize yesterday's traditions in today's schools (Gerstner et al. 1994).

One of the conclusions drawn in the 1983 A Nation at Risk study of our U.S. public education system states, "If an unfriendly foreign power had imposed our schools upon us, we would have regarded it as an act of war" (IBM 1996b, 5). Governor Thompson (Wisconsin) drew a parallel between our academic performance and our performance in the Olympics. We would not consider finishing in 13th or 14th place acceptable for the summer Olympics yet we accept that level of performance in international education rankings.

The following data help define the problem:

- Seventy percent of executives agree that the current educational system is unable to provide them with a sufficient pool of potential employees. Only 3 percent rate the public education system as "excellent" to "very good." High school is seen as the weakest part of the education system (NAB 1997b).
- The majority of Americans say that academic standards are too low in public schools in their own communities and that youngsters are not expected to learn enough. Many feel that a high school diploma does not guarantee mastery of even basic skills (Public Agenda 1994).
- The U.S. mathematics and science curricula are less demanding than those of high-achieving countries. There are fewer classes in algebra, geometry, and calculus, with an over-emphasis on arithmetic and remedial arithmetic (U.S. National Research Center 1996).
- Literacy of the U.S. adult population is, on average, roughly similar to that of the populations in other industrialized countries, but the United States has a greater proportion of adults at the lowest literacy levels (Decker 1997).

- We have treated the education of large numbers of youngsters as a mass-production challenge. But unlike Japan, which graduates 96 percent of its 18-year-olds, we have never reached even 75 percent of our children. Our mass education was and is characterized by very high failure and dropout rates (Gerstner et al. 1994).

NECESSARY SKILLS

In 1991, the U.S. Department of Labor issued a report—SCANS (Secretary's Committee on Achieving Necessary Skills)—that outlined the types of workplace-related skills that all students should possess. These included the abilities to:

- *Manage resources:* productively allocate time, money, materials, space, or staff
- *Work with others:* cooperate with a team, teach others, serve customers, lead, negotiate, and work with diverse men and women
- *Organize and manage information:* use computers and electronic telecommunications hardware and software
- *Work with complex systems:* understand how technical, social, and organizational systems work; monitor; and correct their performance; and design new systems to improve performance
- *Work with a variety of technologies:* select appropriate tools, apply them to the tasks at hand, and maintain and troubleshoot equipment

Effective workers, the report argued, must also possess a foundation that includes:

- *Basic skills:* reading, writing, mathematics (arithmetical computation and mathematical reasoning), listening, and speaking
- *Thinking skills:* creative thinking, decision making, problem solving, seeing things in the mind's eye, knowing how to learn, and reasoning
- *Personal qualities:* individual responsibility, self-esteem, sociability, self-management, and integrity

The report points out that most schools do not directly address many of these competencies or foundation skills. For example, creative thinking, working in groups, and the integration of technologies and tools are seldom part of traditional classroom work.

Although businesspersons sometimes have been accused of wanting to refocus public education strictly on work-related skills, business increasingly needs broadly educated individuals. Today, education for citizenship and for personal fulfillment is much the same as education for economic life because the skills and knowledge needed are the same. The qualities that make a good worker in the modern firm are the same as those that make a good citizen: respect for others, initiative, the capacity to communicate clearly and directly, willingness to take risks while playing by the rules, energy, dedication, and knowledge (Gerstner et al. 1994).

At the National Education Summit in 1996, governors and CEOs from leading U.S. corporations took up the challenge to renew the effort to reform and improve public schools. They agreed on several initiatives, including the need for internationally competitive academic standards and assessments as well as increased accountability for achieving those standards. The governors agreed to drive the standards work, with input from business on what is required in today—and tomorrow's—workplace. Business leaders agreed to require job applicants to demonstrate academic achievement by reviewing transcripts and portfolios. Work is progressing on these initiatives.

Today's workplace requires new skills and places new demands on workers. Traditionally, increases in educational attainment were responsible for an estimated 11–20 percent of growth in worker productivity (Decker 1997). One-third of corporate economists surveyed in 1995 said that their firms were encountering problems in finding skilled labor (NAB 1996). "Corporations do not want K–12 schools to become vocational schools. To the contrary, schools could better serve their students and the business community by producing graduates with higher academic, problem solving and communication skills. We'll teach students how to be marketing people. We can teach them how to manage balance sheets. What is killing us is having to teach them to read and to compute and to communicate and to think" (Gerstner 1996, 5).

American business spends millions of dollars on remediation for what we need employees to bring to the workplace. The American Management Association estimated in 1993 that the average cost per trainee receiving remediation was $244, and the number of American businesses providing remedial training rose from 4 percent in 1989 to 20 percent by 1994.

The nation will need to hire nearly 2 million new teachers over the next decade due to rising student enrollments and growing teacher retirements. "The teachers needed for today's schools must be well-educated and strongly grounded in the liberal arts and sciences with a comprehensive knowledge of the subjects that they teach. Committed to student learning and success, teachers must be able to use a variety of instructional strategies, including IT, to teach children from diverse backgrounds" (Rigden 1996, 1).

STUDENTS' OPINIONS

When students are surveyed, three-quarters believe they would work harder in school if educators expected more of them. Two-thirds admitted they could do better in school if they tried harder. What students say would make them work harder includes:

- having more good teachers (63 percent);
- getting classwork checked and redoing it until it's right (61 percent);
- doing a job internship for school credit (54 percent);
- taking essay tests instead of multiple-choice tests (53 percent);
- kicking troublemakers out of class (53 percent); and
- knowing that more area companies are using high school transcripts to decide who to hire (50 percent).

Students see little connection between their schoolwork and jobs or careers. Most teenagers see little reason to study academic subjects such as history, science, and literature. They view most of what they learn—except for "the basics"—as boring and irrelevant. "The vast majority showed little curiosity or sense of wonder about the subjects they studied in schools. Instead the youngsters slogged through their academic courses, clearing the hurdles adults put in their way, but viewing them as utterly inconsequential to their current or future lives. They found adult insistence that they study them—usually in the form of graduation or college entrance requirements—altogether mystifying" (NAB 1997a, 6).

EXPLOITING TECHNOLOGY IN SCHOOLS

Perhaps the technology revolution begun by personal computers can contribute to a new educational system in which all kinds of children can thrive. Can information and communication technology and its instructional applications impact schools profoundly? Can technology be the basis for new models of teaching and learning and for the changes in behavior necessary for dramatic changes in the results of schooling to occur? It may be possible.

- What if technology that is widely available could eliminate the differences among schools in wealthy and impoverished areas, in urban and rural settings?
- What if technology could stimulate an infinite variety of interests and abilities so learning could thrive and instruction could focus on the removal of barriers from discovery and application rather than on the filling of empty vessels?
- What if technology could enlarge the conversation from a single classroom to conversations among communities, both real and virtual, around the world?

- What if technology could raise the level of education questions and dialogue by engaging world-class participants?
- What if technology could link together homes, classrooms, schools, school districts, and entire states to increase information and communication about student and school performance, expanding the contact time of the school with the students, and improving parent/community support for education?
- What if technology could reduce administrative overhead for teachers and administrators, allowing more time and resources to focus on student needs (Verville 1997)?

Research studies support the use of technology as a valuable tool for learning. It can make a measurable difference in student achievement, attitudes, and interaction with teachers and other students. Important findings were discovered in these studies.

- Educational technology has demonstrated a significant positive effect on achievement. Positive effects have been found for all major subject areas, in preschool through higher education, and for both regular education and special needs students.
- Educational technology has been found to have positive effects on student attitudes toward learning and on students' self-concepts. Students felt more successful in school, were more motivated to learn, and had increased self-confidence and self-esteem when using computers. This was particularly true when the technology allowed learners to control their own learning.
- Introducing technology into the learning environment has been shown to make learning more student-centered, to encourage cooperative learning, and to stimulate increased teacher-student interaction.
- Courses for which networks were used increased student-student and student-teacher interaction, increased student-teacher interaction with lower performing students, and did not decrease the traditional forms of communication used (Sivin-Kachala and Bialo 1994).

HIGHER EDUCATION AND REFORM EFFORTS

There are many ways that higher education can dramatically impact the current K–12 reform efforts, such as:

- improve the academic knowledge of teachers
- develop teachers' integrative skills
- improve the organization and structure of the classroom and school day

- improve the tools utilized in our schools, especially technology
- improve education for administrators

In each of these areas for improvement, research should be undertaken to develop new foundations for teaching and learning models. Too few researchers are studying how people learn and why certain models work, what teaching styles best accommodate various learning styles. Empirical evidence indicates that multi-sensory, interactive, self-directed learning improves understanding and retention. We need the research and scientific foundation that validates the most effective teaching and learning models for today's required skills.

Improve the Academic Knowledge of Teachers

Tomorrow's teachers need to demonstrate strong knowledge in the liberal arts and in their teaching subject areas. A survey from the National Endowment for the Humanities revealed that 77 percent of the graduates of our colleges and universities have never taken a foreign language, 45 percent graduate without studying literature, 41 percent without taking any mathematics, 38 percent have never taken a history course, and 33 percent take no science courses (Rigden 1996). This must change if we are to substantially upgrade the academic standards for public schools. We need to rethink how much of a future teacher's education should come from specific disciplines (math, science, history) versus education theory courses. Clearly balance is required, but today the scale seems balanced away from academics. Minimum requirements for subject-area competence must be established.

Develop Teachers' Integrative Skills

Business critics of the K–12 system focus most strongly on the need for analytical, problem-solving, and communications skills—weaknesses of today's schools. Developing these skills in students will require substantial changes in how teachers are themselves taught. As higher education rethinks the curriculum, clearly the school of education must be a participant. If students in education courses are themselves required to develop, enhance, and continually reinforce communication and problem-solving skills, they will be more capable of helping young people develop those same skills.

Many business leaders have suggested that schools of education and schools of business collaborate in developing programs for future teachers. "As skills needed in teaching come more to resemble those found elsewhere in the workplace, schools that educate teachers must shift toward training that has wide applicability. Teachers need to be familiar with instructional technology; they need training in presentation skills; they must know more about the management of small groups, and be able to assume a variety of leadership roles. Some of these skills may be learned in courses borrowed from schools of business" (Gerstner et al. 1994, 267). These workplace skills have long been required of business graduates, usually learned through case studies and class exercises that could easily be offered to education students.

Teachers must also have more practical experience before they assume responsibility for a classroom of 20–30 children. Once in the classroom, teachers must have the ongoing ability to gain practical experience in new methods or new subject areas. "It's time to reassess the antiquated notion that teachers are 'produced' by one set of institutions (i.e., colleges of education) and 'consumed' by another (i.e., school districts) in isolation from each other" (Rigden 1996, iv).

The National Council for Accreditation of Teacher Education (NCATE) has created standards for professional development schools that identify best practices in integrating internships with professional education. The Holmes Group, created by deans of several schools of education, advocates a five-year teacher education program that combines a solid liberal arts education with extended practical experience in specific professional development schools (Rigden 1996).

"We expect doctors to get training in teaching hospitals. We would not send an NBA player on the court if his only training consisted of lectures on the theory of the jump shot, case studies of the fast break, and films of games played years ago. Why, then, do we entrust our children to teachers who have only listened to lectures, written essays on classroom management and read textbooks on the theory of child development? It's time teachers learned their craft in real schools side-by-side with expert teachers. It's time they got the kind of hands-on experience most other professionals consider vital for certification" (Gerstner 1995, 15).

Improve the Organization and Structure of the Classroom and School Day

We need new strategies to help schools develop the programs that will improve academic achievement. For example, there is clear evidence that parental involvement improves student outcomes. We need to find ways to get parents more active in their children's education and integrated into the education process.

Many classroom models that show promise have emerged in recent years. For example, the New American Schools Development Corporation's model schools are producing exciting results. Although promising, the models have not yet been "scaled up." Rudy Crew, chancellor of the New York City schools, one of the most complex school systems in our country and undoubtedly the largest, says, "Most urban schools have demonstrated the capacity to reform single schools in the individual communities...The real question for urban America is, can you replicate it, can you do it in a cost-effective way and can you create the organizational culture that gives rise to it on a scale that impacts the lives of every child in the system" (Mosle 1997, 32).

That's the challenge. While many districts, large cities, even states, are attempting "scale-up" projects, higher education has a clear role in this area. Working with the successful models, higher education could teach these models in education programs and develop in-service training for other districts.

Improve the Tools Available in Our Schools, Especially Technology

Technology is a key tool in today's workplace. Yet use of technology is very mixed in schools. John Clendenin, chairman and CEO of Bell South, said at the National Education Summit, "We will be inadequate in our response to the competitive education challenge if we do not integrate technology into the classroom. The jobs we're hiring for are technology-driven. If we don't apply technology during the school year, how can we expect our graduates to acclimate to the jobs they aspire to hold?" (IBM 1996b, 11).

Recent studies say more than 90 percent of schools have computers. How the technology is used varies, however. The most frequent computer use by 11th graders was writing papers (Coley et al. 1997). We know that computers are effective, if properly used, i.e., integrated into the teaching process and classroom activities, not as an end in themselves.

The biggest inhibitor to effective use of technology in all classrooms is teacher preparation. Research shows most teachers have no training on the effective use of computers in the classroom. Only 15 percent of U.S. teachers have had at least nine hours of training in education technology, and in 18 states, no technology training is required to obtain their teaching licenses (Coley et al. 1997).

In 1995, a study by the Office of Teacher Assessment found that helping teachers learn how to integrate technology into the curriculum is the most critical factor in successful implementation. Schools of education must ensure that all future teachers are experienced users of technology (Rigden 1996). We must find ways, perhaps through mentor programs and "expert teachers," to provide in-service opportunities for existing teachers to develop these skills.

Improve Education for Administrators

In modern business terms, principals and superintendents are the managers in highly complex, and in many cases, under-performing organizations. They are responsible for establishing the strategies and practices of their schools or districts. Yet most have little or no management training.

In business we know that an outstanding manager can lead a mediocre team to great success; conversely, a mediocre manager will quickly lead an outstanding team to mediocre performance. The overwhelming improvement that is required by our schools necessitates massive restructuring. In business, we call it reengineering—reinventing ourselves by reevaluating all that we do, eliminating unnecessary or unproductive practices, and developing new methods of delivering improved products to global markets. Who does the hard work of reengineering? Senior management. That's the principal and the superintendent in our school systems. We must ensure that they have the training and experience they need to run our most complex enterprises.

CONCLUSION

Today, requirements for workers are substantially different from those of a few years ago; they will be even more different five years from now. This is as true for high school graduates as college graduates. Higher education produces the new research that will be necessary to make the quantum improvements required in our schools. It is also higher education that prepares those who must lead the greatest reengineering mission undertaken by any organization.

The inescapable conclusion is that higher education is a vital player in the reform of our public schools. Aggressive action is required to ensure that those we admit as first-year students and those we hire will be prepared.

Indeed, if we can "fix" our K–12 schools, the benefits will accrue not just to business but to higher education, as well. Improving the education provided to those not college-bound will have an even greater impact on those who become first-year students.

QUESTIONS TO ASK

- How are future teachers being prepared? What is the balance of academics and education theory?
- Do we have effective internship programs where student teachers can practice their profession?
- How do we develop mentoring programs for classroom teachers?
- Is classroom technology an integral part of the teachers' own educational experience?
- Is the School of Education working with other professional schools? Do they gain an understanding of the world their students will enter upon graduation and the skills they will need?
- What programs do we have to help principals/superintendents become effective managers? Do we teach them the fundamentals of reengineering?
- How do we "scale up" the successful models to whole school districts and states?

PART FOUR

• • • • • • • • • • •

Philosophies Guiding Change

CHAPTER 9

Learning as the Core Value

A s business has learned, the focus must be on what customers value. We believe this is a growing sentiment in the academy, as well. There is little question that learning must become one of the core values of business and of society. This also means it must be the core value of the academy.

There is a high cost—to individuals and to society—for inefficient and ineffective learning. The most certain path to individual economic success is a college education. Estimates for the United States suggest that an individual's earnings increase 8–9 percent for each year of educational achievement beyond high school (Jones 1996). Learning leads to higher productivity in business and industry. But are students learning what they need? Does it occur at an appropriate pace? Is our current system as equitable as it should be?

FITNESS FOR USE

We are all supportive of high-quality education. But how is quality defined? The operative definition of "quality" in business and industry is "fitness for use." Transposing this definition on higher education, we will have quality in our educational system when graduates are prepared for the world of work and a balanced life.

As described throughout this book, higher education receives good marks for instilling technical competence in students. However, moving throughout life and career, skills such as communications, problem solving, and the ability to view problems holistically may be more important than implied in school. Although improving, most curricula give little more than lip service to skills such as teamwork and problem solving. Faculty, administrators, staff, and students probably do not share a common understanding of how a quality education would be defined. If we don't know where we are going, how will we ever get there?

The Wingspread Group (1993) defined a quality education as including:

- technical competence in the field
- high-level communications, computational and technological literacy, and information abilities enabling individuals to apply new knowledge as needed
- ability to arrive at informed judgments
- ability to function in a global community
- attitudes such as flexibility, ease with diversity, initiative, motivation, and teamwork
- ability to address complex, real-world problems under "enterprise conditions"

The world students enter will be different. The corollary is that their education should be different. The truth is that most schools have not changed for the worse; they simply have not changed for the better.

When quality is defined as fitness for use, it suggests questions that must be answered to understand higher education's performance and improvement. Are we doing a good job preparing students for careers? Do we understand our processes? Can they be made more efficient? Are we measuring our performance? Are we making our decisions based on data rather than impressions? Any organization that is not asking these types of questions should.

Fidelity between Education and Work

If learning is to be the focus of higher education's activities, and if that learning is to be useful, there needs to be a great deal of fidelity between what is learned and what brings value in the workplace. Today's students learn to read, write, and do calculations, of course, but such basic skills are developed and focused in particular ways. Students often accumulate a large number of facts, yet these facts are not central to their education; they will live their adult lives in a world in which most facts learned years before will have changed or been reinterpreted. In any event, whatever data they need will be available to them at the touch of a computer key (Reich 1991). More important than learning facts is the development of competencies that will have lifelong value.

Analytical versus creative and practical intelligence

To be successful in business—and in life—people need creative and practical skills. However, the development of these skills is often not encouraged in our K–12 system or in higher education. Educational programs tend to focus on analytical intelligence. Does your institution recognize the development of creative or practical intelligence as part of its education objectives? What is your institution doing to develop those abilities in students?

Education must help students understand that they will need these skills. In virtually any business or industry forum focused on business needs, there is discussion of creativity and of the ability to get along. Desirable traits include ones such as "situational relevance," or knowing what to do and how to behave in a given situation (a type of practical intelligence). Particularly in a global economy, different cultures and different values have a large impact on what is correct and what is effective. Another desirable trait is the ability to "connect the dots," to put disparate pieces together to create a whole (a type of creative intelligence using synthesis). Other features relate to looking at the end result, being able to take a holistic view, the ability to interrelate ideas, to create and add value where nothing was before, to be able to put ideas into action, and to understand the unwritten rules of the corporate culture.

We misprepare students if they are allowed to believe that analytical intelligence will be the most important thing in life. While it may be critical to "making the grade," many academic problems are dislocated from people's ordinary experience. How many times have you had to solve a verbal-analogy problem like EVANESCENT: FLEETING:: EPHEMERAL (i) permanent, (ii) long-lasting, (iii) temporary, (iv) instant, in your everyday life (Sternberg 1996, 229)? There are many more realistic problems we can encourage students to solve.

Recognizing and defining problems

In fact, it may be more effective to have students formulate problems for themselves rather than providing them with ready-made problems. "Schools always give kids problems to solve. They are clearly identified as such. They're numbered and have question marks, and they may appear on tests or at the back of book chapters. But real-world problems don't have numbers or question marks, and they occur during the chapters of living, not at the ends. We need to spend much more time helping children (and adults) recognize the characteristics of problem situations and not just assume that our goal is to teach them how to solve obviously recognizable problems" (Sternberg 1996, 157).

Some modifications to the traditional way of doing business are straightforward. Rather than the professor making up the problems for an exam, he or she could assign question-writing to the students. With some assistance and discussion, many will find out that developing problem sets is much more difficult than they imagined. They must be creative. They must understand the subject matter. They must be able to discern which concepts are central and which are peripheral. However, beyond the creativity students must exercise in developing the problem, they will also be developing another important skill: how to define problems.

Successful intelligence, whether at an individual or a corporate level, requires correctly defining problems as much as it requires solving them. In fact, problems cannot be solved unless they are correctly identified. Just as schools give children little or no practice in recognizing problems, they give little or no practice in defining them once recognized. This is the reason so little seems to get done: people spend a lot of time solving the wrong problem (Sternberg 1996).

Another potential activity is to have students analyze a situation and determine if there is a problem. Problem recognition is very important in business. Inability to recognize problems early enough can be deadly. Where in the curriculum do students have the opportunity to develop problem-recognition skills? If they recognize a problem, can they accurately define it? If they can define it, can they create a solution? Can they weigh one solution against another, prioritizing the options?

Approaching ill-defined problems

As important as problem solving is, we must not forget that most problems fall outside the realm of well-defined problems. Much of what constitutes education involves teaching the facts, then testing on those facts. It is a straightforward, well-understood process. Even if students become experts at solving these well-defined problems, they may be missing a great deal. Facts lend themselves to well-structured problems. However, many of the situations found in business and in life are not well structured. Where will students get the experience to deal with ill-defined problems?

We do well in teaching students analytical approaches to solving problems—algorithmic approaches. Often neglected is the heuristic approach to problem solving. Another way to think of heuristics is that they are the "commands" you give yourself to solve a problem. They can include instructions, such as analyze verbally, analyze pictorially, analyze mathematically, draw and label diagram, ask "what if," reexamine knowns/unknowns, reexamine assumptions, let it incubate (Kadesch 1997).

The point is not that problem-solving opportunities do not exist for students, but that often only students at the best schools have the kind of open-ended problem-solving opportunities that prepare them for professional careers. This leaves the majority of learners ill-prepared for the twenty-first century.

Beyond Problem Solving

Systems thinking

Beyond problem solving, education should place more emphasis on systems thinking. Rather than teaching students how to solve a problem that is presented to them, they should be taught to examine why the problem arises and how it is connected to other problems. Learning how to travel from one place to another by following a prescribed route is one thing; learning the entire terrain so that you can find shortcuts to wherever you may want to go is quite another. Students should be taught that problems can usually be redefined according to where you look in a broad system of forces, variables, and outcomes, and that unexpected relationships and potential solutions can be discovered by examining this larger terrain (Reich 1991).

To discover new opportunities, one must be capable of seeing the whole and of understanding the processes by which parts are linked together. In the real world, issues rarely emerge predefined and neatly separable. Students should constantly try to discern larger causes, consequences, and relationships. What looks like a simple problem remedied by a standard solution may turn out to be a symptom of a more fundamental problem, sure to emerge elsewhere in a different form (Reich 1991). How often, in a curriculum built of independent disciplinary pieces, do students have the opportunity to develop this holistic, systems thinking? The solution is not to add another course to the graduation requirement for "Systems Analysis 101."

To learn the higher forms of abstraction and systems thinking, one must learn to experiment. Small children spend most of their waking hours experimenting. Through trial and error they increase their capacity to create order out of a bewildering collage of sensations and to comprehend causes and consequences. But most formal schooling has little to do with experimentation. The tour through history or geography or science typically has a fixed route, beginning at the start of the textbook or the series of lectures and ending at its conclusion. Students have almost no opportunity to explore the terrain for themselves. Self-guided exploration is, after all, an inefficient means of covering ground that "must" be covered. And yet in the best classes of the nation's best schools and universities, the emphasis is on exactly that. Rather than being led along a prescribed path, students are equipped with a set of tools for finding their own way. The focus is on experimental techniques, systematically exploring a range of possibilities and outcomes, making thoughtful guesses and intuitive leaps and then testing them. Most important, students are taught to accept responsibility for their own continued learning (Reich 1991).

Flexible thinking

Even those who develop a systems approach may have difficulty finding creative, effective solutions to problems if their thinking is entrenched. "Many problems are hard to solve because people bring a particular mental set to them—a frame of mind involving an existing predisposition to think of a problem or a situation in a particular way. When problem solvers have a mental set (sometimes called entrenchment) they fixate on a strategy that normally works in solving many problems but does not work in solving the problem at hand. Functional fixedness prevents us from using old tools in novel ways to solve new problems" (Sternberg 1996, 174).

Flexibility of thinking—ways of avoiding functional fixedness—are related to creativity. Flexible thinking—thinking outside the box—is risky. One can often be wrong. It is unfortunate that our educational systems tend to be unforgiving of mistakes. Early on students learn that when they "color outside the lines" they will be corrected. By the time many students reach college age they have learned to not deviate from the norm. This can restrain the development of creative intelligence.

If we want to encourage creativity, we need to include this element in assignments and tests. Sternberg (1996) offers a suggestion. When assigning papers, one could let students know one is looking for demonstration of knowledge, display of analytical skills, and good writing. But beyond that, one could look for and reward creativity. The point is not whether one agrees or disagrees with what they say, but whether they come up with new ideas that represent a synthesis between ideas they have heard or read about and their own ways of thinking.

Tolerance for ambiguity

Another component of creativity is tolerance for ambiguity. Many faculty wish their students had a higher tolerance for ambiguity. Few would not admit to being frustrated by questions about "Will this be on the test?" or "How long does this paper have to be?" In business, many employees are unfit for their positions because of their inability to tolerate ambiguity. Few professions have well-defined job descriptions. Employees are asked to step outside a narrow position description and do whatever is necessary to fix a problem or satisfy a customer's need. There is no course offered in ambiguity tolerance. It is developed through experience with complex, real-world situations. The combination of these "messy" problems with coaching, mentoring, and team support helps individuals develop these skills. Is tolerance of ambiguity a learning objective in any course in one's curriculum? If one asked professionals in one's industry if this is a necessary skill, what would they say?

What else might faculty do? All too often, academic tasks are given to students on a "silver platter." The professor tells one what to do. The textbook gives one a concrete problem to solve. The test asks one a question. One becomes the answer part of a question-answer machine. In the real world, there is no one to serve as the question part. Often, it's not even clear what the question or problem is (Sternberg 1996).

Beyond the question, real-life problems rarely have a single answer. Some answers may be better than others, but the clarity of right and wrong is blurred. Too often academic problems have just one correct response. Although this makes tests easier to grade, it does not develop the kinds of skills that will remain valuable throughout multiple career shifts. Correct-answer tests also fail to take into account differences in values or culture. What might be correct in one culture may be incorrect in another.

LEARNING PRODUCTIVITY

Everyone's time is valuable. If we wanted to measure the productivity of learning, we would be better advised to devote more attention to the learners and their demonstrated mastery of a defined body of knowledge or skills than to seat time or the accumulation of student credit hours. Learning productivity is more important than measures of enrollments, courses taught, or classroom hours assigned. The focus should be less about how to squeeze more out of the faculty than it should be to optimize the learning of students.

One way to make learning more productive is for students to master a body of knowledge in less time. Learning that takes less time can cut the traditional costs carried by the institution, but also the opportunity costs (lost earnings) of the student. Another way to make learning more productive is to make it possible for students to get the courses they need when they need them (Johnstone 1992). If higher education focused on the things that maximize learning—the best curriculum, the best pedagogy, the best learning environment, the most flexibility to adapt to learning styles—learning would be more productive.

"Cognitive scientists tell us what we teachers have long suspected—and long ignored: Different people learn in very different ways and at very different rates. Fortunately, emerging technology promises to help provide just the customization and 'connectivity' that a new educational system would require. We will soon have the opportunity—and the obligation—to adapt courses to the specific cognitive profile of each student, with lectures for those who learn best by listening, sophisticated visual images for those who do better with pictures, and hands-on virtual reality for the many students who learn best by doing" (Langenberg 1997, A64).

PERPETUAL LEARNING

Our educational system ought to have no barriers between its segments, combining "cradle to grave" into one seamless whole. "If we succeed in making the right changes, education will become fully accessible to any appropriately prepared student at any age. We will adapt the delivery of instruction to the student's circumstances, rather than force the student to accommodate to the educational institution's convenience" (Langenberg 1997, A64).

Barriers between segments are too common today. Most of our elementary and secondary schools are designed around an age-graded, assembly-line pattern derived from the "efficient factory" model of the last century. At the postsecondary level and beyond, we've grown accustomed to clear lines of demarcation: corporations do "training," while schools and colleges do "education." Four-year universities educate some, while community colleges educate others. The new economy will blur these lines and prompt the emergence of new structures made up of community colleges, private propri-etary schools, corporate universities, school-to-work opportunities, and cre-dentialed programs. Technology and the new workplace do not respect insti-tutional boundaries. It does not matter what group or which structure is doing the education or the training (Jones 1997b).

Perpetual learning is about more than barriers between types of institutions. Getting educated once is not enough. No two- or four-year (or five- or 10-year) college or university program will ever produce a fully and permanently qualified professional. Perpetual learning is a hallmark of jobs in the new economy. Few can anticipate what competencies or skills they will need a few months or years from today. "A seamless, cradle-to-grave educational system is within our reach, if we muster the courage and the will to create it. That won't be easy, for we have come to believe that our present fossilized educa-tional layer cake and all of its features are somehow eternal and inevitable" (Langenberg 1997, A64).

Are we asking ourselves how to change our methods and forms of delivery as we move from education defined as K–16 to K–life, or lifelong learning? If higher education were to define its market as lifelong learning, our major customers would be employees first and traditional students second. What should be done to reach alumni and other adult learners who need the expertise higher education possesses? Colleges routinely say good-bye to their best customers at graduation rather than turn them into lifelong learners/customers (Davis and Botkin 1995).

INCLUSIVE EDUCATION

If we accept the premise that everyone can be an effective learner, that education is a right in our society, and that we need all the brainpower we can get, our educational system should be more inclusive than exclusive.

Issues of Inclusion

In today's competitive business environment, we need all the good minds we can find or develop. However, it is not always obvious that this is higher education's objective. Alexander Astin challenged higher education to shift its obsession with *being* smart to *developing* smartness in students (Astin 1997). His description of the value of being smart and how it influences the daily lives of academics rings true.

> The most serious consequences of our unexamined emphasis on smartness fall on students. Most of us clearly favor the brightest students, not only in admissions and financial aid, but also in the classroom. If bright students enroll at our institution and take our classes, we believe that this reflects well on our own brightness: surely we must be smart if our students are so smart....The greatest obstacle to well-intentioned efforts to expand educational opportunities for underrepresented groups and to achieve greater equity in our society in general, may well be our obsession with being smart.
>
> The real problem is that we value being smart much more than we do developing smartness. We forget that our institutions' primary mission is to expand students' intellectual capacities, not merely to select and certify those whose intellectual talents are already well developed by the time they reach us. ...educators at all levels want little to do with students who do not get high scores or grades. But our country's future probably has more to do with how effectively we educate such students than with almost anything else we do. We need to commit ourselves— individually and institutionally—to develop and nurture those skills, both in our students and in young faculty members. (Astin 1997, A60)

Too many of our institutions operate on an exclusive rather than an inclusive basis. "Just when we need more people with more education coming into the workforce, we are seeing signs of support for a movement that would have just the opposite effect. I believe we must stop such thinking dead in its tracks. It will deprive our country and our state of the educated workforce both need to remain economically competitive. Further, it will deprive many people of the high quality of life they would otherwise enjoy" (Brand 1997, 402).

There are other impediments to an inclusive educational system. A study of barriers to participation in education and training programs found that non-participants are deterred by situational barriers such as personal problems, lack of confidence, lack of time, or education costs. Structural barriers (policies or practices of organizations that discourage participation) often cited by part-time students were admission and financial aid policies, availability of advisers in the evening, and class scheduling. Adult students want to spend their campus time inside classrooms and not waiting in lines; they want practical applications of classroom material (Goal 5 Work Group 1993).

Even though education should be more inclusive, not everyone is college material. "That isn't a value judgment; it's the truth" (Harwood 1997, A19). Eighty percent of jobs in the American economy don't require a four-year college degree and that situation is not expected to change significantly anytime soon. But many of these jobs do require basic skills that vast numbers of high school students are not getting. These skills—including math and reading comprehension, oral communication, and word processing on computers—can be taught in high school. They would add enough value to a high school diploma to command a wage of $30,000 a year or more (Harwood 1997).

Costs of Exclusion

In the second chapter we described the importance of education to business and society. The 1997 Council for Aid to Education study reveals alarming trends about the financial consequences of turning qualified people away from higher education because of cost or access. Most agree that education is the key to economic competitiveness and social stability. We cannot afford to turn away less desirable students. It makes little sense morally or economically. The remedy may lie in funding formulas and reward structures—not the existing ones, but ones yet to be devised.

Many institutions still adhere to a "weed out" philosophy, irrespective of the selectivity of admission. Notorious are first-year engineering programs, pre-med programs, etc. To some faculty, it is a point of pride that theirs is the "killer course" that eliminates those unfit to move on. Have they considered that those who do not make it in our system may well be replaced by individuals from other countries?

There is an economic result of the weed-out philosophy, as well. As Brand explains:

> In Indiana the breakeven point for state services is $38,000. The average Indiana worker who earns less than $38,000 uses more services than he or she pays for through taxes. Someone who earns more than $38,000 contributes to the general tax revenue above the average state expenditures per capita.

In Indiana, the average high school graduate earns $34,000 and the average college graduate earns $55,000 per year. Thus, the average college graduate is likely to be a net contributor to the public welfare, whereas someone without a college degree is apt to be a net user of services. It is to the benefit of the state to increase the proportion of the population obtaining college degrees. (Brand 1997, 403)

ASSURING ACCESS FOR ALL

Technology is a required competency in the workplace. Scholarship has been transformed by computers through techniques such as visualization and collaboration. Yet many institutions are unwilling to mandate technology competency as a graduation requirement or the purchase of computers as part of the cost of an education. Without an institutional commitment to IT, we risk building a society of haves and have-nots.

There is evidence that this is already happening. Students with the means to purchase computers are doing so (national estimates are 50+ percent). These students have a significant advantage over those who must rely on computer labs where waiting lines and outdated equipment are more often the rule than the exception. Mobile computing (student possession of laptop computers) can help ensure that all students have equal access to technology (Oblinger, Mingle, and Resmer 1998).

While student ownership increases the cost of a student's education, it is not disproportionate to other expenses accepted as reasonable educational costs. Students typically spend around $200 per semester on textbooks. Purchasing a $1,600 computer, paid for over four years, represents a similar level of investment (Heterick 1994). The potential benefits are at least as great. However, adding a cost of this magnitude to existing educational expenses may price some students out of the market. For this reason, any program must recognize and provide for the special needs of these individuals (Resmer, Mingle, and Oblinger 1995).

Over the next decade, perhaps the most important of the many public policy issues associated with the emerging information society is to make sure that everyone has an opportunity to benefit from IT and its virtually limitless potential. To do so will require assuring access for all.

Ideally, we all would have access to IT with an affordable, ubiquitous connection to the network computing world. Citizens everywhere could access education and communicate with government agencies, health care providers, community organizations, businesses, family, and friends. Universal access would enable parents to learn about their children's daily homework assignments and to communicate regularly with teachers and school administrators. Students would be able to gather information from distant libraries, research centers, and global peers.

Even though more schools have PCs, colleges and universities are expanding computer support, and 60 percent of the homes with children under seven have a computer, some are still left out. Perhaps the most practical way to make network services available is through public access facilities located in community-based institutions such as schools, libraries, health clinics, post offices, and community centers. However, the biggest contribution that state and local authorities can make toward promoting universal access to IT is to ensure that school curricula — from elementary school through university — expose students to networked services and train them in the use of IT. In the emerging information society, students and adults who do not know how to exploit the Internet and its capabilities will be at a serious disadvantage.

The have/have-not issue is broad. We must significantly improve access to affordable, high-quality learning for traditionally underrepresented and undereducated students and adults. We can ill afford the loss of talent of those who are geographically isolated or economically disadvantaged, or workers and students with different learning styles. The need for human capital in our society is immense. We cannot afford to miss the opportunity to develop human potential by allowing some learners to remain disenfranchised. It is essential that the next generation understand the technology so they can employ it on the job and in their daily lives.

CONCLUSION

For business to be successful, learning must become the core value in education. This means we must become more focused than ever on what students will need and how our institutions can best provide it. Assuming that what worked today will be sufficient for tomorrow is a going-out-of-business strategy. The financial and human repercussions of allowing learning to be haphazard or to be a second (or third) priority are not acceptable. Knowledge and learning represent one of the only sources of sustainable advantage in a fast-moving, highly competitive world.

CHAPTER 10

The Enlightened Organization

I f higher education is to adapt and evolve in response to the rapidly
changing needs of its constituents, many of its traditional structures and
policies—designed in an era of stability and incremental change—may be
insufficient to deal with the challenge. How higher education conceptualizes
itself, structures the organization, and handles its financing as well as how it
measures itself (and its competitors) will either help or hinder its ability to
serve society.

THE BUSINESS OF HIGHER EDUCATION

One of the unique features of higher education is that it operates based on
public trust. Perhaps because of this trust, higher education less frequently
articulates answers to questions that are posed to other organizations. However, the questions are still relevant.

- What is your business?
- What is your top priority?
- Who must you please? (e.g., customers, owners, shareholders, regula-
  tors, others?)
- What is your relationship to the community?
- Who are you going to reward and how? (On what will that reward be
  based? Seniority? Merit? Innovations? Bottom-line results?)
- What is the long-term vision of the organization?

Can one succinctly articulate the fundamental purpose—"the business"—of higher education? Of one's particular institution? Would a faculty member's statement be the same as a board member's? How similar would the statements of a student and a staff member be? Although everyone would be able to state a purpose, it is all too likely that there would be great divergence in emphasis.

Questions such as "What is your business?" or "What is your top priority?" are not simple. Although platitudes may come easily (e.g., "The students are our top priority"), are they really the truth? If instruction is the top priority, do funding and reward systems reflect it? Do students feel that they are the institution's top priority? If a college or university feels that it serves the community, how often is the organization in dialog with the community? When asking for suggestions from advisory groups, is action taken on the advice or is it filtered because "we know best"?

In business, we often ask, "What business are you in?" The question is frequently skirted by academics because many assert that higher education is not a business. With revenues and assets in the millions and earnings from endowments resulting in net worth increases of up to $2 billion a year, many outside the academy have difficulty rationalizing this denial. "A major obstacle [to change] is the unwillingness to recognize that a college or university can no longer claim to be like a snug little boarding school community and the concomitant unwillingness to accept the fact that colleges and universities are organizations, and often large, complex, expensive ones at that. The main point is not to prod the contemporary university to behave more like a business, but to nudge it to behave more like an organization. Or better, to get it to behave like an organism that must feed itself, change and adapt to its environment" (Keller 1983, 173–74).

There are actually multiple businesses in the "business" of higher education. Today these functions are aggregated in the traditional structure of the college or university. If the evolution of higher education follows the integration of value chains, such as is occurring in other industries, there will be the opportunity to disaggregate some of these functions.

The Knowledge Business

Hague (1996) contends that higher education must shift its roles. "If universities are to be effective in the twenty-first century, they will need to recognize that the university is a (nonprofit-making) knowledge business with two main roles. It will itself produce knowledge through research and, even more important, encourage studies to interpret research." He asserts that the value of "scholarship—interpreting fields of other people's research rather than just research on one's own—is inadequately recognized in most universities, while 'original' research (even if not very original) has too high a status" (Hague 1996, 5).

The Customization Business

Universities will conduct their knowledge business in a world where the "industrial model" of education, with large numbers of people taught the same things in the same ways, will become increasingly unacceptable because it is increasingly unnecessary. Developments in information and communications technology will mean that hardly any students will need to follow exactly the same educational model and that colleges and universities can allow for students' individual learning styles. Teachers will have to adapt by spending more time as advisors/mentors rather than as lecturers. Their role as tutors will be a crucial one (Hague 1996).

The Content Business

Others describe providing content as one of the "businesses" of higher education. Among the most striking features of the current educational model is the enormous duplicated effort that goes into the production and presentation of the same courses in thousands of locations with marginal reuse or sharing of efforts. Tate (1995) calls for the development of production, delivery, and certification organizations (PDCs) that would operate on a national basis, using the most efficient and effective communications media available. Courses and programs would be designed and produced to commercial standards. These organizations would purchase subject-matter expertise from many sources, depending upon the degree of expertise and the quality of the content required.

The Brokerage Business

Electronic commerce and education brokerages could broker, market, advertise, and process customer applications for education offerings (Hamalainen et al. 1996). Able to match customer needs with existing and prospective courses available from any number of educational suppliers, they could also accommodate requests outside the mainstream by bringing in educators with special expertise or through customized combinations of course elements.

The Certification Business

Either within structures such as Tate's PDCs or in independent certification organizations, competence-based testing and certification services would be provided. Students could participate in interactive testing at any time or at a place of their choosing—and pay a fee to receive certification upon successful completion.

The Credit Bank Business

Langenberg (1997) contends that a universal college credit banking system will evolve. Students will demonstrate their mastery of certain skills at different points in their lives and will receive certificates of achievement. Together these certificates would create a "performance profile" that might replace the traditional curriculum vitae.

The potential benefits of these new models for education go beyond more convenient access to education and the ability to customize courses according to customer needs. They may dramatically alter the cost structure of education. As education brokerages leverage their ability to mass-market their product to customers around the globe, it is conceivable that they will be able to achieve an unprecedented economy of scale that might drastically reduce the unit cost of what colleges and universities commonly charge today.

These "components" of higher education can be aggregated, as they are in existing institutions, or disaggregated, as they are in emerging organizations such as the Western Governors University (WGU). Western Governors University will provide degrees, certificates, and learning-on-demand, but most of what it offers will be provided by others. Operating as a consortium or brokerage where members of the consortium provide services from which students may choose, the permanent staff and physical facilities are minimal. Western Governors University will "broker" courses and services from multiple educational providers spanning both the public and private sectors. Learners and providers of courses, programs, and learning modules will be linked. Assessment services will be provided—both online and in local offices. Students will be able to customize entire postsecondary programs that best suit their individual needs (Leavitt 1997). The intent is for WGU to be customer-driven, focused on the needs of the learner, and a cost-effective means of providing skills, competencies, and knowledge to learners without necessarily replicating the traditional structure of existing institutions.

As these new models are being considered, the nonprofit/for-profit status of higher education should be rethought. In their book, *For-Profit Higher Education: Developing a World-Class Workforce*, Sperling and Tucker (1997) make a case for the creation of more for-profit, adult-centered universities. In their view, the advantages of a for-profit entity extend to all stakeholders in the education enterprise. Among the advantages of for-profit universities are

- they pay federal and state income taxes and local property taxes;
- they have access to private capital for funds needed for startup and/or expansion and therefore can respond rapidly to changing and growing needs;

- two of their goals are growth and profit—goals that, over time, can be achieved only by producing a high-quality service that meets the needs of the customer;
- they are managed to deliver a service at a given level of quality at the least cost, and a system of faculty governance and close links to external stakeholders helps to ensure that they meet the advertised quality standards (Sperling and Tucker 1997).

We need to be careful not to assume that education is synonymous with place and physical facilities, such as schools, campuses, residence halls, and library buildings (Connick 1993). Neither is it synonymous with the existing organizational or operating structure or profit/nonprofit status. All of these can be allowed to vary. What is important is the fundamental purpose of postsecondary education and how well it achieves its mission. Education is learning; it is knowledge, information, skills, abilities, and personal development. But that doesn't necessarily happen at a particular place or as a result of a predefined organization chart.

Business needs higher education to take a fresh, unbiased look at whether the way its business is transacted is the best model or merely the most familiar. Could strategic alliances, value chain integration, and new business models result in more and better learning?

FINANCIAL MODELS

The most common criticism of higher education is that its costs are out of control. Higher education budgets have grown at rates from two to six times the consumer price index (CPI) for more than 20 years. In *Breaking the Social Contract*, the Council for Aid to Education (1997) describes the impact of this financial crisis. "What we found was a time bomb ticking under the nation's social and economic foundations. At a time when the level of education needed for productive employment is increasing, the opportunity to go to college will be denied to millions of Americans unless sweeping changes are made to control costs, halt sharp increases in tuition, and increase other sources of revenue" (CAE 1997, 2).

Given current trends in both funding and the costs of higher education, the deficit in operating expenses for the nation's colleges and universities will have quadrupled by 2015. Assuming tuition increases no faster than inflation, by that year U.S. colleges and universities will fall $38 billion short (in 1995 dollars) of the annual budget they need to educate the student population expected in 2015. If, however, tuition increases at current rates—basically doubling by 2015—the impact on access will be devastating: effectively half of those who want to pursue higher education will be shut out.

Beyond total cost, there is criticism regarding the taxpayer costs of higher education. Sperling and Tucker (1997) estimate that taxpayers subsidize $6,428 of the annual expenses for every student who attends a public institution of higher education. The figure is $5,773 per annum of each student's expenses for attending a private institution. Perhaps most striking is the figure of $1 billion that taxpayers paid in 1995 to send 161,000 talented undergraduates to the nation's 50 most expensive private colleges and universities. If taxpayers had the opportunity to decide whether they subsidized this expense today, would they?

As higher education gains more public attention, figures such as these are likely to increase demands for change. If educators respond by simply asking for more funds, they are unlikely to be successful. Institutional reform, according to the Council for Aid to Education (1997), is a prerequisite for increased public funding. Unless the higher education sector changes the way it operates by undergoing the kind of restructuring that successful businesses have implemented, it will be difficult to garner the increases in public funding needed to meet future demands.

To get a sympathetic ear from legislators, higher education will need strong advocacy from the business community, an ally it is unlikely to win unless it has put itself through the same sort of streamlining and reengineering that the business community has implemented to reduce costs and improve service. However, with the existing financial and governance structures, higher education may be unable to change. In a highly fragmented system where governance is based on consensus, it is difficult for anything to change. (Who would vote to reduce or eliminate one's own program in favor of someone else's?) In addition, the funding patterns of higher education are based on the past, not the future. The best projection of next year's budget is to look at last year's. When considering the need for change and its rapidity, this is an archaic model. Today, institutions each raise all the money they can, spend all they get, and spend it in ways that relate closely to the way they spent the money the previous year. How can an institution adapt to change when it is nearly impossible to reallocate funds due to permanent personnel, departmental allocations, line-item budgeting, and institutional inertia?

The governance structure of higher education is part of the problem. The decision-making units, policies, and practices that control resource allocation have remained largely unchanged since the nineteenth century. Designed for an era of growth, the current structure is cumbersome and even dysfunctional in an environment of scarce resources. To make it worse, only a few college administrators can provide cost-per-unit-of-service statistics for each of their education programs (Sperling and Tucker 1997). Impediments to change are built into the management assumptions and practices of colleges and universities.

Another financial dilemma is posed by the number of ancillary activities that are bundled into the cost of education. "In economic terms, the mission-critical activity of higher education is the production of degrees to specified standards of quality, quantity and cost. Other activities of higher education—such as research, sports and joint ventures—should be accounted for separately. As principles of accounting and accountability, we should never commingle the costs of those activities with mission-critical activities. A root cause of higher education's current problems is that its organizational structure and information decision-support systems are wholly inadequate to meet modern needs or to adapt to new needs that will emerge in the future" (Sperling and Tucker 1997, 52).

What is needed now is a systemwide process for reallocating resources among departments and other parts of the institution. Just as successful companies have learned to focus on their core competencies—the products and services they supply at a better quality and lower price than their competitors—higher education institutions and systems need to reexamine their missions and streamline their services to serve those missions. This task requires that operations be seen from a broad perspective, one that will lead to such questions as: Which of our centers, departments, colleges, or services enjoy comparative advantage over those of other education or training institutions? Would another classics professor contribute to the educational mission more than another mathematics professor? More than acquiring additional equipment for the geophysics laboratory? More than expanding the student counseling program? More than repairing classroom and dormitory roofs? (CAE 1997)

Finding answers for these types of questions will require not only a new decision-making process, but a concerted effort to generate data on the costs and benefits of providing different services. With the structure as it is now, decision makers have not had to choose among competing functions, so comprehensive information systems have not evolved to support such decisions. Higher education officials simply do not have the information they need to compare missions and functions and understand the trade-offs among the potential allocations being considered.

Measurement systems must improve. This will entail instituting performance-based assessment, defining and measuring productivity, and integrating accounting systems. Once this information is available, higher education's next step will be to alter the governance system so that decision makers can make choices based on the relative value of departments, programs, and systems in order to reallocate scarce resources. Even if the data were available today, governance structures would rarely allow action to be taken.

Higher education will need to develop better ways of knowing how much specific activities cost and what their relative merits are, then making the difficult decisions that will undoubtedly be required to keep costs under control. The funds colleges and universities spend are not just their own. The taxpayers and businesses who help subsidize higher education will increasingly demand accountability in return for those dollars.

ORGANIZATIONAL MODELS

The inherited organizational structure of higher education may be a significant impediment to change in the academy. Within those institutions created in the last decade (e.g., CSU-Monterey Bay, Florida Gulf Coast University), a number of "standard" features are missing. Tenure is not necessarily part of the employment expectation. Multidisciplinary teams are common. Student services are aggregated rather than separated into discrete units.

"American scholars have, to their glory, forged some valuable knowledge about organizations, group psychology, planning and management. This knowledge should not remain inert, unused. It is applicable to colleges and universities, who need all the aid they can get against the troublesome period ahead. Faculty professionals should see that enlightened academic executives who are employing the new knowledge to cope with fiercer conditions are not a freshly armed enemy but activist colleagues" (Keller 1983, 174).

From what perspective should we view the work of the organization? Many of our existing organizational structures are more historic than rational. Work is performed in "functional silos." Vertical organizational structures preserve internal order but do not necessarily serve the learner. These vertical silos, (for example, admissions, registration, bursar, financial aid) are hierarchical in nature. They have managers and supervisors to review and approve the work of others. When staff in a given department (e.g., admissions) complete a task, (e.g., admit a student), they hand it off to another work group where the next set of specialized tasks is performed (e.g., register the student, process financial aid applications, etc.). This model of student services delivery, more the norm than the exception today, produces frustrated students who wait in lines and who cannot request and receive the information they need from a single source or in a timely manner.

The work—specific tasks—that many employees perform have nothing to do with meeting customer needs; they are done to satisfy the internal demands of the organization, hence the world of multiple reviews, four-part forms, and approval signatures. Often things are done simply because they have always been done that way. Higher education must redefine administration, eliminate unnecessary work, dismantle unproductive practices, and redesign policies to improve efficiency and effectiveness.

One of the first steps in such a process is to focus on the work to be done. Organizations evolve not just because they change but because we change our point of view in looking at the work of an organization. For almost any process on campus, it is probable that our view of that work today is different than when the process was put in place. We need to redefine the work. To meet the needs of students, more and more work will be directed by cross-functional and self-governing teams. The effectiveness of such teams will depend on their members' access to one another, to cross-functional information, and occasionally, to elements of the campus leadership. Departmental boundaries and fiefdoms will get in the way of work.

Organization charts are an example of an administrative practice that has decreasing relevance. Although they are useful guides, organization charts are outmoded. Institutions do not manage through structures anymore, they manage through processes. The emergent organizational structures succeed by empowering people and horizontal processes in ways that are supplemental to—or independent of—the "formal" vertical organization. Competing for, winning, and administering a grant crosses multiple boundaries—the graduate school, the research division, the finance office, the department(s) of the principal investigators, graduate students, postdoctoral candidates and undergraduate assistants, IT, library, office of technology transfer and industry research, etc. Recruiting and admitting students involves multiple offices— enrollment management, student services, academic affairs, financial aid, assessment services, housing, IT, alumni affairs, and more. The web-like connections among these organizations are how work gets done. The hierarchy gets in the way.

To enable organizational transformation, we need to shift our attention away from the organization chart and toward the creation of an information-rich infrastructure and connections among people. We will need to eliminate the technical, cultural, hierarchical, and procedural boundaries that divide or isolate intelligent and motivated people. We should promote easy access to the kinds of information people need for making sound decisions and we should create a policy environment that stimulates and rewards collaboration. Finally, we must specify, measure, and reward the achievement of defined and customer-centric objectives (Ernst et al. 1996).

STRENGTH FROM STRATEGIC ALLIANCES

New kinds of strategic alliances will be required for higher education to remain competitive in the twenty-first century. A greater sharing of resources— courses, services, infrastructure, libraries—could lead to significant savings and improved services. Outdated notions (e.g., philanthropy equals partnership) must disappear. Business, industry, alumni, and parents can make positive contributions to education. However, before they can, partnerships and strategic alliances need to be redefined.

VALUE FROM ALLIANCES

The Competitive Advantage

The competitive advantage of an organization grows out of the value that it creates for its buyers, whether those buyers are students, employers, or the government. Porter (1985) asserts that the competitiveness of an organization depends on five factors:

- bargaining power of buyers
- bargaining power of suppliers
- the threat of new entrants
- the threat of substitute products and services
- rivalry among existing firms

There are a number of trends that are making higher education more competitive; many relate to technology and the emergence of hundreds of in-person and online educational providers.

As educational options expand, students can exert more power by exercising their options. If not satisfied with local or regional postsecondary education suppliers, they can go elsewhere, perhaps choosing online alternatives. Some colleges and universities have enhanced their power as suppliers by putting in place mobile computing initiatives or guarantees on degrees. Technology has allowed many new entrants to higher education. In fact, publicly traded educational corporations are doing well. To further expand the number of competitors, some industry organizations are defining competencies and developing curricula, not always requiring that the educational provider be part of the academy. Indications are that the competitiveness in postsecondary education will become intense.

In business, and increasingly in higher education, competitive advantage results from strategic alliances. Higher education should establish strategic alliances with potentially important future suppliers—hardware and software vendors, telecommunications companies, publishers, and others. Just as no one person has all the skills needed for a job, no single institution has all the skills it requires. Strategic alliances among higher education institutions and partnerships with business and industry will become increasingly common in the future. The trend is already apparent in the growing number of consortia, buying cooperatives, and shared service agreements that exist.

In some cases, strategic alliances will be created so that key personnel may remain focused on the core competencies of the institution. Although operating a mailroom, the bookstore, or a computer system is part of running the university, none of these represents the university's core business. Instruction and research are the core businesses. On a sliding scale ranging from "insourcing" to "outsourcing," universities have the opportunity to select which activities to "own" and which to contract out to other providers.

Perhaps the Internet is the biggest threat. Thousands of individuals and institutions now have the chance to dabble in the business of supplying distance education. The entry barriers are low. Technological change is expanding the boundaries of the distance education segment of the education and training industry. It has already done so geographically. By enhancing the quality and attractiveness of courses, it will bring more customers into the market. The widening set of interrelationships among distance education and the media, computing, and communications industries presents more opportunities than threats to universities (Daniel 1996).

The Western Governors University (WGU) is an example of reconceptualizing the business of higher education and making use of strategic alliances. Leavitt (1997), one of the founding governors of WGU, reminds us that today information and knowledge flow wherever the people are, unlike the situation in the industrial age, when people had to go to campus to get information. The educational monopoly which existed for some 2,000 years is broken. In the twenty-first-century digital age, as learning becomes a lifelong pursuit, there will be so many different sources and opportunities to gain knowledge and learning that in some cases the seat-time, credit-hour measurement system will be obsolete. Instead of trying to hold back the onslaught of education and training opportunities, we should develop strategic alliances and sophisticated assessment methods to bring the best options and the highest quality experiences to the learner.

Increased Opportunities for Exchange

There are other ways in which business and higher education can work together. It is no longer tenable (if indeed it ever was) to accept a practice in which a university "educates" a student to some level of competence and thus having done its job and "completed" its task, turns this finished product over to an employer to do with as may be fitting. It will be imperative that we form effective partnerships between industry and academe for education and training.

One component of such a partnership might be the short-term exchange of personnel. Inbreeding ultimately weakens a species. It has weakened many businesses and can weaken higher education, as well. The careers of many faculty have been exclusively within higher education institutions. The preferred career path is to move from a bachelor's to a Ph.D. degree, then on to a faculty position without leaving the confines of the academy. For a fortunate minority this presents no impediment because a variety of external contacts—such as consulting—keep them in touch with how their disciplines are practiced in the world outside. For others, however, the insularity of the academy can be ossifying. Just as we believe students benefit from study-abroad opportunities and internships, wouldn't faculty benefit from substantive contact with business and industry?

It is a human tendency to fear or dislike the unknown and unfamiliar. This may account for why the attitudes of faculty are often divided along the lines of those who have the most contact with the outside world. For example, liberal arts faculty, who often have little contact with business personnel, are inclined to insist that job preparation is not their concern, that the university was created as an independent critic of the larger society, and that the life of the mind need not be sullied by the world of commerce and finance. Many representatives of this group are openly hostile to business. Professional school faculty, however, tend not only to be sympathetic to the needs of business, but at many institutions they also have made substantial curriculum modifications in response to such needs (ACE 1997).

Employees' most caustic comments about their education are reserved for courses, activities, and professors considered to be largely disconnected from the work world and, therefore, a waste of their time. A consistent theme—whether they had majored in the liberal arts, business, or engineering—was a desire for more courses offered by professors who had hands-on experience in the business world rather than purely theory-based knowledge (ACE 1997).

Institutions such as the University of Phoenix specifically choose to hire faculty who are working professionals. They believe that effective education for working adults requires instructors who bring their knowledge and skills from the workplace to enable those who are less knowledgeable and less skilled to make immediate improvements in their work performance (Sperling and Tucker 1997).

Students benefit from increased contact with external experts. When they graduate, a valuable skill will be the ability to locate and obtain information from experts. In many institutions, students learn—by default—to rely on faculty as their "experts." While this may be adequate during college, it will become less viable with time. Involving external experts throughout the college experience benefits the learner, the faculty, and the expert. Students develop a larger network and can seek guidance from faculty in assessing the quality of these experts. The faculty have the opportunity to share some of their work load as well as to learn from others. Many alumni and interested professionals are very willing to donate time to colleges and universities.

Whether higher education seeks to bring external experts into education or not, the students are already seeking them out. Thanks to online resources, students routinely consult others. Who cannot cite an example of a student who based a substantial amount of a term paper on the advice of someone they located over the Internet? One of the impacts of online access is a shift in the relationship between a professor, a textbook, and a student. At one time, this triad was prevalent. Students now can have access to a number of professors, a number of other experts, and an almost unlimited supply of textual as well as visual information. Those who would limit students' contacts to the professor and a textbook are denying reality.

From a variety of perspectives, the conclusion is that industry continues to be an underutilized partner in the education process. Faculty need to become more familiar with the practice of their disciplines in business and in industry. University administrators and faculty members need more knowledge of what business does, how it does it, and what their graduates need to know to function effectively in a business or industrial environment.

Conversely, too few in business and industry have an adequate understanding of how our colleges and universities currently function, how the faculty reward system works, or the constraints under which faculty members must operate. We should greatly expand faculty-industry exchange programs. The objective of such programs would be to provide faculty and administrators with first-hand knowledge of industry practice and issues, which would allow them to devise curricula that are truly responsive to industry needs. In addition, we should consider industrial post-doctoral internships as requisites to tenure-track academic positions (McMasters and Matsch 1996).

There are a number of specialized programs that exemplify business-university cooperation, such as the Global Wireless Education Consortium (GWEC). Global Wireless Education Consortium was organized to meet the projected employment needs of almost 300,000 technicians and engineers for the wireless industry by 2007 and employs 30,000–50,000 of those workers today. Between 250,000 and 270,000 wireless employees will need to be hired within 10 years—many of whom will be technicians and engineers. Speed of curriculum development is important. The normal development of a textbook may be two years. Wireless technology changes monthly. Therefore, GWEC is helping develop curricula and curriculum "accessories" for daily learning processes, and it also provides ongoing learning opportunities for faculty and students. Global Wireless Education Consortium is just one example of where a business-university partnership has moved beyond philanthropy to where members of the alliance contribute unique skills that ultimately benefit students and the economy.

POLICIES

To create an enlightened organization, policies must be aligned with stated goals, objectives, and practices. All institutions claim that teaching and learning are top priorities. At the same time, few disagree that tenure and/or promotion are jeopardized by focusing on quality teaching or the incorporation of technology into the curriculum. In a 1992 report to the National

Science Foundation entitled "America's Academic Future," young faculty members summed up a complaint heard from all quarters: "Tenure guidelines uniformly denote that teaching, research, and service are the criteria for tenure. It is our experience, however, that the road to tenure is marked research, research, research" (Coye 1997, 24).

The changes required across higher education will not occur without a shift in the reward structure. The response to a very human question, "What's in it for me?" must be clearly articulated. Similarly, when administrators who promote well-reasoned change encounter career-threatening resistance, there is little hope of alternatives developing within the academy. Organizations produce the very things they reward and pay attention to. Does higher education have the performance measures or incentives needed to become more competitive?

There are regulatory constraints, as well.

> Few needed reforms in higher education will be initiated without removing the existing barriers that protect higher education from the natural consequences of its actions, consequences it would experience were it to operate fully or even largely in the marketplace. It is regulation that keeps higher education out of the learning experiences of the marketplace and allows it to develop unrealistic, often counter-productive standards and practices. The regulators of this fragmented market—accreditors, state agency officials, and a variety of federal officials—have constructed capital- and labor-intensive 'input' standards that they believe, usually with little justification, will ensure that the education offered by institutions they license or accredit will have value. Those input standards include not only specifications on physical plant, faculty, and seat time per credit, but a prohibition on paying anyone based on their success in recruiting or retaining students.

> Although monetary incentives for performance are now accepted as the primary engine that will improve productivity in business and, increasingly, in progressive not-for-profit and governmental organizations, we have banned these incentives from higher education. This is bad public policy. (Sperling and Tucker 1997, 57)

The issue of rewards and regulations is broader than individual security and compensation. Many campuses believe, philosophically, that courses and resources should be shared. However, if a department or an institution develops a course that is offered to other campuses, where is their reward? Today, many of our state university systems have regulations that prohibit the department offering the course from receiving compensation for the student credit hours the course generates off-campus. If sharing a course simply generates extra work and bureaucratic hassles, where is the benefit in sharing expertise or resources? The problem extends beyond student credit hours within a system. If department X seeks to "market" their unique degree to another institution, the revenue generated from department X goes into the general fund. The department does not benefit from its efforts.

At the same time that colleges and universities are withholding rewards, they are allowing other opportunities to slip away. Most often it is faculty who are teaching on-campus in a traditional setting who are receiving additional compensation for teaching online for a competing institution during their "off hours." Other faculty are developing online courses as works-for-hire that are owned by other institutions, some of which are outside of the United States. Individual faculty are entrepreneurial, developing their skills and marketing their expertise to other institutions when their home institution does not offer the incentives necessary to keep the intellectual capital within the institution. Such short-term inflexibility in reward structures is likely to have a negative long-term impact.

Probably the most visible, incongruous college and university policy to the outside world is tenure. It is under fire across the country. Many view tenure as the single biggest impediment to change in higher education. The tenure system is regularly blamed for many of the perceived ills of higher education, including:

- the inability of universities to dismiss unproductive faculty
- the inability of universities to reorganize
- an undue focus on research at the expense of teaching
- faculty loyalty toward professional organizations at the expense of their institutions
- a prevalence of individual fiefdoms
- the high cost of higher education

The level of job security enjoyed by faculty, further, is said to be unjustified relative to that of other sectors of the economy (Gilliland 1997).

Most businesses gave up the notion of guaranteed employment in the last decade. It represented a difficult adjustment; no one wants to give up job security. But from the point of view of customers and stockholders, it is a justifiable policy. The rationale is that if you do not bring value to the business, the business does not owe you a paycheck.

External to higher education, many wonder why faculty in higher education merit guaranteed employment. As job security has evaporated for more and more Americans, there is a growing question of why professors are different. Even if the public accepted that tenure was still a relevant policy (a.k.a. the preservation of academic freedom), who would be chosen to vote on it? Today other faculty determine who is tenured and who is promoted. This is contrary to the notion of serving customers. In most other sectors of society, those determining tenure would comprise a more representative sample of those who the faculty member was to serve, encompassing feedback from students and employers as well as other faculty.

Whether the symptom is tenure, intellectual property, or rewards, the cure will depend on policy. Compared to the magnitude of change facing our institutions, the creative rethinking of policies is rare.

> Why is the pace of innovation so slow in higher education? Why is there so little leveraging of higher education's intellectual and material resources to gain productivity? Why is there not wholesale exploitation of the new information technologies to produce more efficient educational models—including the for-profit adult-centered model? Why are the same technologies not exploited to assess the processes and learning outcomes of education and, ultimately, to assess their impact on the workplace and the economy? The most under-explored answer to those questions relates to excessive regulation and state control of the structure and processes of higher education. (Sperling and Tucker 1997, 56)

Some 3,700 small, medium, and large public and private colleges and universities operate under the rules of more than 65 accrediting associations, 50 state licensing agencies, and, increasingly, the U.S. Department of Education, the U.S. Department of Defense, and the Veterans Administration. An excess of regulation in higher education makes it difficult, often impossible, for institutions to innovate and thus they are unresponsive to the rapidly changing needs of society and the economy (Sperling and Tucker 1997).

More recommendations for deregulation are being heard than ever before. The rationale is that deregulating higher education will allow a wide range of providers to develop and deliver content to specific standards. At the same time, accountability to the public and to student consumers needs to be established (Twigg and Heterick 1997). Deregulation and accountability will be difficult concepts for higher education. However, the time for avoiding either may be past.

MEASURABLE CRITERIA

Higher education appears to acknowledge that legislators and the public are increasingly critical of college and university systems. It is not colleges' and universities' fundamental role that is the issue. Both groups are acutely aware of the need to train labor to keep their economies competitive, and they are coming to recognize the value of colleges and universities as engines of economic development. However, there is a perception that higher education is often wasteful of taxpayer money. "It is small consolation that this waste is not attributed to malice but to lax management, minimal accountability and the inertia of doing things as we have always done them. We do not frivolously spend money on things that do not benefit our states. We do, however, spend money on things that benefit our states far less than others might" (Hooker 1997, 23).

Over the past decade, demands for accountability have begun forcing institutions to measure their performance and communicate it to stakeholders. Even though many have begun, more needs to be done to measure and communicate outcomes and the "added value" of the educational process. Demands for increased productivity arise from the common perception that faculty do not teach enough, students do not learn the right things, and administrators are reactive "firefighters" instead of effective managers. And the high fixed costs of doing business (e.g., aging, decaying infrastructures, and massive deferred maintenance) give institutions a hefty bill to pay regardless of the number of students they attract and retain (Hafner and Oblinger 1998).

"Higher education rarely deals with the goals of instruction directly and has avoided stating them in measurable terms. Institutions have been much more comfortable measuring the quality of their institutions by indirect indices (degrees held by faculty, faculty publications and honors, grant dollars, etc.) than by what students have learned. Indirect measurements of quality avoid the inevitable fact that once you have stated your goals in measurable terms, you become accountable for assessing how well you are meeting those goals and for making difficult decisions if you are not doing so" (Diamond 1997, B7).

"If we believe that our high school graduates can and must demonstrate through 'performance' measures that they meet high educational standards, we should be able to embrace the same ideas for students of any age. If we can do that, we stand a fighting chance of creating an educational system through which all our citizens move smoothly and efficiently, at rates limited only by their intrinsic abilities, building richly detailed performance profiles as they go. These profiles will be far more informative indicators of students' capabilities than mere diplomas and degrees" (Langenberg 1997, A64).

Beyond the performance of individual students, the "health" of the institution is a concern. An effective measure of institutional performance should provide a holistic view of the institution. One of the most effective tools to address measurement and accountability is the "balanced scorecard" (Kaplan and Norton 1996), which integrates vision, goals, measures, and controls. Performance indicators take into account the customer perspective (e.g., how students or legislators regard the institution), an internal business process perspective (e.g., cycle time, use of resources), a financial perspective (e.g., revenue, expenditures), and an innovation and learning perspective (e.g., asking how well the institution is improving and creating value or how well the students are succeeding in their chosen professions).

Measurements help people better understand what is happening. They help people communicate that insight to each other, to legislators, to parents, and to students (a form of accountability). Measurements help us gain insight into what really needs to change and how well we are doing (Cortada 1998). Few institutions will significantly improve by chance. Those with well-articulated objectives that are linked to appropriate measures are more likely to excel than those without them.

CONCLUSION

Business will need to be more creative, agile, and quick. If higher education is to meet the needs of businesses and employees in this rapidly evolving environment, it will also have to become more creative, agile, and quick. This will require the creation of an enlightened organization that sees both itself and the future differently. These future-focused organizations will be less hierarchical and more heavily based on a web of interactions than are today's educational institutions. By implication, the structure, functions, organizations, procedures, and policies of this enlightened organization will be different from the traditional models in place today.

If we do not develop more future-compatible organizations, the risk is that education will become less and less affordable just as it becomes a necessity for more of our citizens. The economic and social consequences of excluding more Americans from postsecondary education would be grim. The alternative is to reconceptualize the "what" and "how" of the "business" of higher education.

CHAPTER 11

Welcoming Change

T he rate of change in our world will not slow anytime soon. If anything, competition in most industries will speed up over the next few decades. Enterprises everywhere will be presented with even more wonderful opportunities and with dire hazards, driven by the globalization of the economy along with related technological and social trends. The structure, systems, practices, and culture of the typical twentieth-century organization have often been more of a drag on change than a facilitator. If the current rate of change continues, the standard organization of the twentieth century will likely become a dinosaur (Kotter 1996).

THINKING IN THE FUTURE TENSE

Being Comfortable with Change

The first step, for both business and higher education, is to be honest—with ourselves and with each other. Change is disconcerting, uncomfortable, and frightening. Few of us are so objective that when we are criticized or hear a litany of weaknesses we do not take it personally or rush to the defense. Defensiveness aside, couldn't we all do better?

In business, ignoring criticism can be fatal. That has not necessarily been true for higher education. In almost every setting, we have heard faculty, staff, administrators, and others argue for the preservation of the status quo. Many of the arguments sound selfish. Why would anyone who has a secure, stable job advocate change? Others are active proponents of change. Whether we advocate or resist change, whether we are in business or in education, the days of stability and security are probably already gone. Denial may be deadly—not just for business but for higher education. There is no question that if higher education does not change, business and our economy will suffer.

Preparing for Tomorrow

The world is moving so rapidly that being prepared for today simply isn't good enough. James (1996) asserts that business needs people who can *think in the future tense.* "You need to understand how the currents of technological change will affect your life and your work, how economic changes will affect your business and its place in the global market, how demographic and cultural changes will alter your self-perception" (James 1996, 24). She lists skills such as perspective, cultural knowledge, flexibility, vision, energy, intelligence, and global values— skills that have been described throughout these chapters.

It is a good list for business. We should be asking ourselves how many of our staff, line managers, and executives exhibit these qualities. It is also a good list for higher education. How many undergraduates possess these attributes? How many Ph.D. candidates? Do boards look for these attributes in presidents and chancellors? What would a curriculum that fostered the ability to "think in the future tense" look like?

Higher education should be concerned with the rate of change. As business increasingly measures change in Web years (three months equals a Web year), higher education will need to quicken the pace of change. Although proud of its stability, its challenge will be to redesign itself to welcome constant change. Change is predicted on multiple fronts.

- **Redesign of education.** Because of dramatic technological advances, education is entering one of the most challenging and potentially creative periods in its history. The computer revolution has created entirely new educational tools that can be used not only to transmit information but also to enrich human interaction. These new tools challenge the educational establishment to rethink itself and rethink education as well. They challenge people and institutions that have long been good at preaching change to practice it themselves (Farrington 1997).
- **Flexible faculty.** Universities must create and sustain a professional faculty workforce that is flexible and highly productive. Not every instructor needs to be a tenured faculty member (Brand 1997). The future may dictate that we will need fewer full professors. There will be a tendency on the part of many faculty to resist change in order to protect their jobs, but market forces will have a stronger say (Hooker 1997).

- **Increased efficiency.** Colleges and universities must enhance their efficiency, effectiveness, and accountability. All must adopt the best practices, especially in business operations. They should be run as efficiently as the best corporations. Additionally, universities should stick to their core businesses, and contract for other services (Brand 1997).
- **Removing boundaries.** Market realities and new pedagogical imperatives will have other far-reaching implications for the internal structure of colleges and universities. Technology will lead to increased research and teaching across disciplines. Traditional boundaries will break down.
- **New markets.** Universities should seek additional opportunities in the sale of their educational services. We in higher education must be as entrepreneurial and creative as any industry (Brand 1997).

Changing higher education begins with setting aside current assumptions about how the college/university operates and for whom. When institutions succeed in challenging their current assumptions and in redefining them, the picture that emerges is surprisingly different.

Area of Transformation	Current Assumptions	New Focus
Instructional mission	Task to teach	Task to enable learning
Human resources	Select talent	Develop talent/skills
Strategic focus	Budget-driven	Goal-driven
Market focus	Students	Customers
Value to student	Degree by courses	Student learning outcomes/competency
Organization	Working hierarchy	Networked groups
Worker focus	Manage hierarchy	Teams
Rewards	Loyalty/seniority	Performance
Resources	Physical assets	People value
Competitive indicator	Institutional	Student achievement budget/reputation
Governance	Faculty autonomy	Collective responsibility
Size	Growth	Right-sized
Scale of delivery	Large	Flexible
Competition	Regional	National/global

CHALLENGING PARADIGM PARALYSIS

Questioning Tradition

What assumptions does an institution need to challenge or what assumptions does a department or unit need to reassess? For example, if we focus on learning, there are many "traditions" that we might question. Where is the proof that 120 credit hours of instruction merits a baccalaureate? What does the baccalaureate degree certify? How did we come to believe that 50-minute lectures, three times a week, was optimum for all of our students? What caused educators to decide that the length of the semester should be constant while student learning is allowed to vary (Hooker 1997)?

Challenging our own assumptions is only a starting point. Among our off-campus constituencies of parents and alumni we may need to stimulate a paradigm shift, as well. The scoring systems used to rank colleges and universities are based on measures such as volumes in the library, student/faculty ratios, numbers of full professors, etc. In the digital age, volumes in a campus library are less important than access to worldwide resources. A numeric score for student/faculty ratios is less meaningful than the quantity and quality of the interactions that occur. It is more important to ask whether competency has been gained than from whom students learn or how much time was spent. We need to define the true measures of quality so we can break away from ratings that reinforce the past instead of the future.

Looking for the Added Value

One of the most significant changes brought about by IT is that it places pressure on the "middleperson." Computer networks offer the possibility of the consumer directly accessing services and information rather than going through an intermediary. We have already seen these pressures in business. A common thread among automatic teller machines (ATMs), travel information, and online stock transactions is that the network makes the "middleperson" potentially superfluous. People and businesses thrive only when they add value to the process. Fewer and fewer survive by mediating a transaction.

It is too easy to assume that a process adds value because it has always been done that way. To search for the added value ask:

- How does this step in the process add value to the whole?
- Could we eliminate this activity if some prior activity were done differently?
- Could this activity be eliminated without affecting the final product or service, from the customer perspective?
- Is this activity required by the customer and will the customer pay for it?

New ways of conceptualizing a process can reduce time and expense as well as focus on the value-added portions. For example, consider a typical travel expense reimbursement process with an average cycle time of three weeks. Potential problems within the process include mathematical calculation errors, currency conversion mistakes, missing signatures, travel expense coding errors, and incorrect routing. Analysis of the travel expense reimbursement process often reveals a high degree of "non–value-added" activity—steps in the process that have no value in the eyes of the customer. This process can be redesigned by eliminating the steps that contributed no value, and by introducing new technology and work policies to expedite the process. The redesigned travel expense reimbursement process reduces cycle time from three weeks to three days, reduces errors, eliminates unnecessary reviews and approvals, and places the money directly in the employee's account (Hafner and Oblinger 1998).

One of the challenges to higher education will be to identify those "transactions" where humans are "in the middle" as opposed to those in which they add value. For example, some higher education institutions are finding that a large percentage (up to 60 percent) of student inquiries for information (e.g., financial aid, overdue parking tickets, etc.) can be handled by an information system; only a modest percentage require human intervention. "One-stop shopping" service centers or Web interfaces allow students to get the information they need through a convenient, customer-oriented approach. Institutions using such philosophies are discovering that the result is a reduction in the amount of time students need to conduct business transactions as well as an improvement in customer services and satisfaction. In addition, staff time can be refocused on higher value activities such as establishing a financial plan for the cost of a student's education or determining how to incorporate an internship into their program of study.

CULTURE OF CHANGE

Even though the rate of change is becoming a defining feature for business, industry, and education, change will not "take hold" until the organization's culture and its beliefs evolve. Many cultural changes are already occurring in higher education. Institutions speak of "customers." There are discussions about learning organizations. Total quality management (TQM) and reengineering are no longer foreign concepts. Higher education has changed throughout our history—land-grant institutions were created, the community college movement began. Societies change, cultures change, expectations change, and so do our organizations.

To decide whether an institution has developed a culture of change, ask:

- What do the leaders pay attention to and talk about? Identify their actual priorities versus what gets lip service.

- How are rewards and status determined? Does performance—as measured by external customers—make a difference or is it more important to conform to the norms of those inside the organization?
- What is the nature of the organization's structure, systems, and procedures? How long is the rule list? How dense are the regulations?
- How does the organization respond to a crisis? Is there cooperation or is there a rush to maintain individual, "pet" projects?
- Is there support for team building and risk taking?
- How do the formal statements of organizational philosophy compare to reality (James 1996)?

Why Transformations Fail

Most of us would probably conclude that our organizations have a long way to go in developing a culture of change or in transforming ourselves. Kotter's *Leading Change* (1996) details the most common reasons why transformations fail.

Complacency

One of the most important deals with complacency. By far the biggest mistake people make when trying to change organizations is to plunge ahead without establishing a high enough sense of urgency. This error is fatal because transformations always fail to achieve their objectives when complacency levels are high. It is hard to drive people out of their comfort zones. Unfortunately, complacency in higher education is high. Too much past success, a lack of visible crises, a lack of performance standards, and insufficient feedback from external constituencies all add up to complacency. Without a sense of urgency, people cling to the status quo and resist initiatives to change.

Lack of Vision

Another element is a vision. Vision plays a key role in producing useful change by helping to direct, align, and inspire actions on the part of large numbers of people. Without an appropriate vision, a transformation effort can easily dissolve into a list of confusing, incompatible, and time-consuming projects that go in the wrong direction or nowhere at all. Without a vision to guide decision making, each and every choice employees face can dissolve into an interminable debate. In many failed transformations, we find plans and programs trying to play the role of vision. Books spelling out procedures, goals, methods, and deadlines will not substitute for a sensible vision.

Poor Communication

Once you have a vision, people must know about it. Major change is usually impossible unless most employees are willing to help. Without credible communication, and a lot of it, people's hearts and minds are never captured.

Although some organizations develop a good vision, they under-communicate it by addressing the vision at only a few meetings or sending out a few memos. At other times the head of the organization communicates the vision, but his or her vice presidents, deans, and department chairs are virtually silent. Passive resistance can kill a transformation effort. It is important to remember that communication comes in both words and deeds. Nothing undermines changes more than behavior by important individuals that is inconsistent with the verbal communication.

Obstacles

There will be many obstacles in the way of change. A frequent one is organizational structure. Narrow job categories or unchallenged self-interest can undermine efforts to improve services and make programs more responsive to learner or employer needs. All too often, compensation or performance appraisal systems force people to choose between the new vision and their self-interests. How often do we hear of senior faculty advising new tenure-track assistant professors to minimize teaching and avoid getting involved with IT projects or student clubs because research is the only thing that really counts in getting tenure? If the change effort does not confront these organizational obstacles, success is undermined.

Fixed Culture

In the final analysis, change occurs only when it becomes "the way we do things around here," when it seeps into the very bloodstream of the department or collegial body. Until new behaviors are rooted in social norms and shared values, they are always subject to degradation as soon as the pressures associated with a change effort are removed. Two factors are particularly important in anchoring new approaches in an organization's culture. The first is a conscious attempt to show people how specific behaviors and attitudes have helped improve performance. When people are left on their own to make the connections, they can easily create inaccurate links. Anchoring change also requires that the next generation really does personify this approach. If our institutions believe that teaching and learning should be different, is it reflected in the training of Ph.D. candidates? In the position descriptions of faculty? In the promotion and tenure guidelines for the institution?

Supporting Change

What modifications will need to be made for higher education to thrive on change rather than resist it?

- If the rate of external change continues to climb, then the urgency rate of the winning twenty-first century organization will have to be medium to high all the time. The twentieth-century model of lengthy periods of calm or complacency being punctuated by short periods of hectic activity will not work. A higher rate of urgency does not imply ever-present panic, anxiety, or fear, however. It means a state in which complacency is virtually absent, people are always looking for both problems and opportunities, and the norm is "do it now."

- In a fast-moving world, teamwork is necessary almost all of the time. In an environment of constant change, individuals, even if supremely talented, won't have enough time or expertise to absorb rapidly shifting disciplinary, pedagogical, and technological information. They won't have enough time to communicate all the important decisions to others. They will rarely have the charisma or skills to single-handedly gain commitments to change from large numbers of people. Teams will be essential.
- In the twentieth century, the development of professionals—in the classroom and on the job—focused on management. People were taught how to plan, budget, organize, staff, control, and problem solve. We must now develop leaders—people who can create and communicate visions and strategies. Management deals mostly with the status quo; leadership deals mostly with change. We must become more skilled at creating leaders.
- Complex skills, such as leadership, emerge over decades. Development of leadership potential does not happen in a two-week course or a four-year college program. Lifelong learning is essential if people are to develop these complex skills.

If one is hoping to let the next generation lead this change, remember that there are others in the industry who have created adaptive cultures and are developing awesome competitive machines (Kotter 1996). Perhaps the strongest impetus for change will be the realization that higher education must be the architect of change rather than its victim. "We must shape our own destinies aggressively or policy makers will do it for us" (Gee 1994, 22).

COMPOUND GROWTH

The key to creating and sustaining the kind of changes business and higher education need in the twenty-first century is leadership—not only at the top but throughout the organization. Leadership is not just something a chosen few are born with. Leadership is heavily intertwined with lifelong learning.

Leadership and lifelong learning are closely related to the power of compound growth. Those who become leaders don't give up. They learn from good experiences and bad ones. They watch and listen. They test new ideas, even when it means pushing themselves out of the "comfort zone." Listening with an open mind, trying new things, reflecting honestly on successes and failures—none of this requires a high IQ, an M.B.A. degree, or a privileged background. Yet remarkably few people behave in these ways today. In spite of this fact, some people keep growing while others level off or decline. As a result, those who push themselves out of the "comfort zone" become more and more comfortable with change (Kotter 1996).

> Consider a simple example. Between age thirty and fifty, Fran "grows" at the rate of 6 percent—that is every year she expands her career-relevant skills and knowledge by 6 percent. Her twin sister, Janice, has exactly the same intelligence, skills and information at age thirty, but during the next twenty years she grows at only 1 percent per year. Perhaps Janice becomes smug or complacent after early successes. Or maybe Fran has some experience that sets a fire underneath her. For Fran and Janice, the difference between a 6 percent and a 1 percent growth rate over twenty years is huge. If they each have 100 units of career related capability at age thirty, twenty years later, Janice will have 122 units while Fran will have 321. Peers at age thirty, the two will be in totally different leagues at age fifty. (Kotter 1996, 181)

The habits of lifelong learners are relatively simple. They take risks and try new ideas. While most of us become set in our ways, they keep experimenting. They honestly reflect on their successes and failures and learn from them. They solicit opinions from others. They don't make the assumption that they know it all or that others have little to contribute. Much more than the average person, lifelong learners listen carefully and do so with open minds. In the short term, these habits may be uncomfortable, but in the long term they are the source of growth (Kotter 1996).

NEED FOR LEADERS

Times of rapid change require leaders. Yet, to most outsiders (and many insiders) campuses still look the same. The subjects are the same, the format and delivery are similar, and people are hired the same way. In general, change has not been welcomed.

New patterns in the economy, demographics, government spending policies, the use of technology, and the expectations of students and their families assure that higher education will never be the same. "Political and corporate America have already responded by fundamentally restructuring the way they operate. We in higher education are only now beginning to face this momentous challenge. To be sure, we have been tested before, but the combinations and intensity of pressure, in a context of shrinking resources and fading public confidence, constitute a genuine crisis. Indeed, one of our problems is that business and elected leaders believe ever more strongly that the pace and intensity of their remodeling dramatically outstrips ours," according to Munitz (1995, 22).

He contends that higher education must design search processes and professional training programs that bring to higher education's chief executive officer positions people who understand and are comfortable with concepts of public accountability, consumer and client expectations, relationships be-tween pricing and access, and the balance between traditional faculty expec-tations and contemporary social requirements. If higher education fails to do this it will be unable to remain competitive. "The only way we will have leaders who are imaginative, courageous and professionally trained will be to depart from higher education's traditional view of presidential responsibility as 'the last bastion of amateur management'" (Munitz 1995, 42).

CONCLUSION

To make welcoming change a part of our future, we will need to ensure that change and experimentation become the norm within our institutions rather than being reserved as necessities to be used during crises. Leadership will be required to create a clear vision, to develop coalitions, and to ensure that attention is focused on the most important priorities over the long term. Episodic and short-lived initiatives must give way to a more holistic approach. Part of welcoming change is recognizing that the many external (and internal) forces affecting our institutions will continue to demand mid-course correc-tions. Perhaps most importantly, welcoming change will require the active engagement and leadership of the faculty. If faculty are to be able to respond to the challenges of the future, they must play an intimate role in recognizing and responding to change.

There is no single blueprint for what higher education should do to better serve society and business. The university of the twenty-first century will be created with vision, planning, execution, and common sense. Our institutions have strengths we would not want to abandon. In addition, we must consider human nature—we are rational as well as emotional beings. Changes in one aspect of the institution can have a ripple effect throughout other parts of the institution. Even the finest plans may fail without sufficient application of common sense.

We have posed some difficult questions throughout this book. We hope they cause business and higher education to challenge existing assumptions. The point is not that our past has been wrong or bad. The point is that the future will be different. It is only by asking these difficult questions that higher education will retain the position of importance to society that it has enjoyed in the past.

BIBLIOGRAPHY

Altbach, Philip, and Peter Maassen. 1997. Faculty attitudes: International perspectives on the academic professions. Forum for the Future of Higher Education, 21–23 September, Aspen.

American Council on Education (ACE). 1995. Educating Americans for a world in flux: Ten ground rules for internationalizing higher education. American Council on Education, Washington.

———. 1996. Higher education and work readiness: The view from the corporation. Task Force on High Performance Work and Workers: The Academic Connection, Washington.

———. 1997. Spanning the chasm: Corporate and academic cooperation to improve work-force preparation. Task Force on High Performance Work and Workers: The Academic Connection, Washington.

Astin, Alexander. 1997. Our obsession with being smart is distorting intellectual life. *The Chronicle of Higher Education*, 26 September, A60.

Backhaus, Kara, and Charles Whiteman. 1994. The regional impact of the University of Iowa. Institute for Economic Research, University of Iowa.

Bardwick, Judith M. 1996. Peacetime management and wartime leadership. In *The Leader of the Future: New Visions, Strategies, and Practices for the Next Era*, edited by Frances Hesselbein, Marshall Goldsmith, and Richard Beckhard. San Francisco: Jossey-Bass Publishers, 131–39.

Beck, Melinda. 1997. The next big population bulge: Generation Y shows its might. *Wall Street Journal* (3 February). <http://interactive4.wfj.com/archive/r...link.tmpl&id=>.

Beede, Martha, and Darlene Burnett. 1998. Student centered services for the 21st century: Creating the student centered environment. In *The Future Compatible Campus*, edited by Diana Oblinger and Sean Rush. Bolton, Mass.: Anker Publishing Company, 68–86.

Bennis, Warren, and Patricia Ward Biederman. 1996. *Organizing Genius: The Secrets of Creative Collaboration*. Reading, Mass.: Addison-Wesley Publishing Company, Inc.

Bivins, D. Lawrence. 1998. Managing innovation: Project implementation in higher education. In *The Future Compatible Campus*, edited by Diana Oblinger and Sean Rush. Bolton, Mass.: Anker Publishing Company, 230–46.

Bluestone, Barry. 1993. UMass/Boston: An Economic Impact Analysis. January. Unpublished.

Bothun, G. D. 1996. Teaching via electrons: Networked courseware at the University of Oregon. *CAUSE/EFFECT* 19, no. 4 (winter):37–43.

Brand, Myles. 1997. Some major trends in higher education: Limited-access model vs. opportunity-driven model. *Vital Speeches of the Day* 63, no. 13 (7 February):402–5.

Broad, Molly Corbett. 1992. Leveraging technology for the strategic advantage of the university. Claire Maple Memorial Lecture, Seminars on Academic Computing, 10 August, Snowmass, Colo.

Brown, John Seely, and Paul Duguid. 1996. Universities in the digital age. *Change* 28, no. 4 (July/August):11–19.

Carlsen, Mary Baird. 1991. *Creativity and Aging: A Meaning-Making Perspective*. New York: Norton Publishing Company.

Cavusgil, S. Tamer. 1993. Internationalizing business education: Defining the challenge. In *Internationalizing Business Education*, edited by S. Tamer Cavusgil. East Lansing: Michigan State University Press, 1–13.

Chickering, Arthur W., and Stephen C. Ehrmann. 1996. Implementing the seven principles: Technology as lever. *AAHE Bulletin* 49, no. 2 (October):3–6.

Coley, Richard, John Cradler, and Penelope Engel. 1997. Computers and classrooms: The status of technology in U.S. schools. Policy Information Center, Educational Testing Service, May, Princeton.

Connick, George. 1993. Beyond a place called school. Presentation to the President's Development Council, 20 January, University of Maine, Orono.

Cortada, James W. 1998. Knowing how it is all working: The role of performance measurements. In *The Future Compatible Campus*, edited by Diana Oblinger and Sean Rush. Bolton, Mass.: Anker Publishing Company, 248–71.

Council for Aid to Education (CAE). 1997. Breaking the social contract: The fiscal crisis in higher education. Santa Monica: RAND.

Coye, Dale. 1997. Ernest Boyer and the new American college: Connecting the disconnects. *Change* 29, no. 3 (May/June):20–29.

Daniel, John S. 1996. *Mega-Universities and Knowledge Media: Technology Strategies for Higher Education*. London: Kogan Page Limited.

Davis, Stan, and Jim Botkin. 1995. *The Monster Under the Bed*. New York: Simon and Schuster.

Decker, Paul T. 1997. Findings from education and the economy: An indicator's report. NCES 97-939. U.S. Department of Education, National Center for Education Statistics, Washington.

Diamond, Robert M. 1997. Curriculum reform needed if students are to master core skills. *Chronicle of Higher Education*, 1 August, B7.

Dillman, Don A., James A. Christenson, Priscilla Salant, and Paul D. Warner. 1995. What the public wants from higher education: Workforce implications from a 1995 national survey.

Dolence, Michael G., and Donald M. Norris. 1995. Transforming higher education: A vision for learning in the 21st century. Society for College and University Planning.

Drucker, Peter. 1994. The age of social transformation. *Atlantic Monthly* (November): 53–80.

Duderstadt, James J. 1996. Toward an educational transformation, winter, University of Michigan, Ann Arbor.

Eisenberg, M. B., and D. P. Ely. 1993. Plugging into the net. *ERIC Review* 2(3):2–10.

Ellsworth, Jill H. 1994. *Education on the Internet*. Indianapolis: Sams Publishing.

Ernst, David, Richard Katz, and John Sack. 1996. Organizational and technological strategies for higher education in the information age. CAUSE Professional Paper Series, no. 13, Boulder.

European Community Information Society Project Office (ECISPO). 1995. Adaptation of education and vocational training systems. <http://www.oecdwash.org/PRESS/PRESRELS/communic.htm>.

Farrington, Gregory. 1997. Higher education in the information age. In *The Learning Revolution*, edited by Diana Oblinger and Sean Rush. Bolton, Mass.: Anker Publishing Company, 54–71.

Fisher, George M. C. 1990. A customer's view: World-class corporate expectations of higher education. *Educational Record* (fall): 19–21.

Fletcher, J. D. 1991. Effectiveness and cost of interactive videodisc instruction. *Machine Mediated Learning* 3: 361–85.

Forman, D. C. 1995. The use of multimedia technology for training in business and industry. *Multimedia Monitor* 13 (7): 22–27.

Gee, E. Gordon. 1994. Universities must be the architects, not the victims, of change. *Springfield* (Ohio) *News Sun*, 21 August.

Gerstner, Louis V. Jr. 1995. Remarks at the National Governors' Association Annual Meeting, 30 June, Burlington, Vt.

———. 1996. Remarks at 1996 National Education Summit.

Gerstner, Louis V. Jr., Roger D. Semerad, Denis Philip Doyle, and William B. Johnston. 1994. *Reinventing Education: Entrepreneurship in America's Public Schools*. New York: Dutton Publishing.

Gilliland, Martha W. 1997. Organizational change and tenure: We can learn from the corporate experience. *Change* 29, no. 3 (May/June):30–33.

Goal 5 Work Group. 1993. Reaching the goals: Goal 5. Adult Literacy and Lifelong Learning, U.S. Department of Education, Washington.

Graham, Ellen. 1997. Generation Y: When the terrible twos hit their terrible teenage years. *Wall Street Journal*, 5 February.

Green, Kenneth C. 1996. The changing profile of undergraduate business students. *Journal of Career Planning and Employment* (spring) 21–26.

———. 1997. Drawn to the light, burned by the flame? Money, technology and distance education. *ED Journal* 11, no. 5 (May): 1–9.

Group of Seven (G7). 1996. G7 Jobs Ministerial Conference, 1–2 April, Lille, France. <http://ut12.library.utor...cuments/g7/lillejobs.htm>.

Hafner, Kris, and Diana Oblinger. 1998. Transforming the academy. In *The Future Compatible Campus*, edited by Diana Obinger and Sean Rush. Bolton, Mass.: Anker Publishing Company, 2–23.

Hague, Douglas. 1996. Options for the future. Paper for CVCP Private Seminar on Universities and the State, January. Unpublished.

Hall, James W. 1995. Educational technology initiative: Greeting the dawn of a new millennium. Empire State College. *CLT News* 1:1.

Hamalainen, Matti, Andrew B. Whinston, and Svetlana Vishik. 1996. Electronic markets for learning: Education brokerages on the Internet. *Communications of the ACM* 39, no. 6 (June):51–58.

Harasim, Linda. 1991. Teaching on-line: Computer conferencing as an educational environment. Proceedings of the International Symposium on Computer Conferencing, June, Ohio State University, 16–27.

———. 1993. Collaborating in cyberspace: Using computer conferences as a group learning environment. *Interactive Learning Environments* 3(2): 119–30.

Harasim, Linda, Starr Roxanne Hiltz, Lucio Teles, and Murray Turoff. 1995. *Learning Networks: A Field Guide to Teaching and Learning On-line.* Cambridge, Mass.: MIT Press.

Harvey, Lee, and P. T. Knight. 1996. *Transforming Higher Education.* Buckingham, England: Society for Research into Higher Education (SRHE) and Open University Press.

Harvey, Lee, Sue Moon, and Vicki Geall. 1997. *Graduates' Work: Organizational Change and Students' Attributes.* Birmingham: Centre for Research into Quality, The University of Central England.

Harwood, Richard. 1997. Lost in the job market. *Washington Post*, 9 September, A19.

Hersh, Richard H. 1997. Intentions and perceptions: A national survey of public attitudes toward liberal arts education. *Change* 29, no. 2 (March/April):16–23.

Heterick, Robert C. Jr. 1994. The shoemaker's children. *Educom Review* 29, no. 3 (May/June):60.

Hooker, Michael. 1997. The transformation of higher education. In *The Learning Revolution*, edited by Diana Oblinger and Sean Rush. Bolton, Mass.: Anker Publishing Company, 20–34.

IBM Corporation. 1990. A vision of IBM resource performance in the year 2000. Armonk, N.Y.: IBM Corporation. Internal publication.

————. 1993. *Fundamentals of Project Management: Course Handbook.* Purchase, N.Y.: IBM Corporation. Internal publication.

————. 1996. Social exclusion, technology and the learning society. Purchase, N.Y.: IBM Corporation. Internal publication.

————. 1996b. A review of the 1996 National Education Summit. Armonk, N.Y.: IBM Corporation. Internal publication.

————. 1997. Protecting our health and safety. <http://www.ibm.com/ibm/publicaffairs/health/index.html>.

Information Technology Association of America (ITAA). 1997. Filling the gap: IT workforce challenges and solutions. Unpublished.

Jaeger, George. 1991. Description of a freshman computer class taught completely on-line by computer and modem, hosted on BBS spring/fall 1990. *ED Journal 5*, no. 4 (April):8–13.

James, Jennifer. 1996. *Thinking in the Future Tense.* New York: Simon & Schuster.

Johnstone, Douglas B. 1992. Learning productivity: A new imperative for American higher education. *Studies in Public Higher Education.* Albany: SUNY.

————. 1994. College at work: Partnerships and the rebuilding of American competence. *Journal of Higher Education 65*, no. 2 (March/April): 168–82.

Jones, Dennis. 1996. The promise of technology-based instruction: What are we learning? *NCHEMS News 13* (March): 2–4.

Jones, Robert T. 1996. The impact of workforce quality in the new American economy. Testimony of Robert T. Jones on behalf of the National Alliance of Business before the Subcommittee on Trade, Committee on Ways and Means, U.S. House of Representatives, 25 June. <http://www.nab.com/legislation/issues/quality.html>.

————. 1997a. The challenges ahead for the business community. <http://www.ba.com/news/jones.html> (26 March).

————. 1997b. How workplace demands are driving workforce policy. <http://www.nab.com/legislation/issues/demands/html>.

Kadesch, R. R. 1997. *Problem Solving across the Disciplines.* Upper Saddle River, N.J.: Prentice Hall.

Kangas, Ward Randall. 1997. Incremental tax revenue effects of higher education. University of Illinois at Urbana-Champaign. Unpublished.

Kanin-Lovers, Jill. 1997. Personal communications.

Kanter, Rosabeth Moss. 1996. World-class leaders: The power of partnering. In *The Leader of the Future: New Visions, Strategies, and Practices for the Next Era,* edited by Frances Hesselbein, Marshall Goldsmith, and Richard Beckhard. San Francisco: Jossey-Bass Publishers, 89–98.

Kaplan, R. S., and D. P. Norton. 1996. *Translating Strategy into Action: The Balanced Scorecard.* Cambridge, Mass.: Harvard Business School Press.

Karrass, Chester L. 1974. Give and take: The complete guide to negotiating strategies and tactics. New York: Thomas Y. Corwell.

Kearsley, Greg, William Lynch, and David Wizer. 1995. The effectiveness and impact of on-line learning in graduate education. *Educational Technology 35*(6): 37–42.

Keller, George. 1983. *Academic Strategy: The Management Revolution in American Higher Education*. Baltimore: The Johns Hopkins University Press.

Kennedy, Donald. 1995. Another century's end, another revolution for higher education. *Change* 27 (3): 8–15.

Kindleberger, Richard. 1997. Study: MIT at root of 4,000 firms. *Boston Globe*, 3 March.

Kotter, John P. 1996. *Leading Change*. Boston: Harvard Business School Press.

Kramer, G.L. 1996. Developmental academic advising. National Academic Advising Association, July, Summer Institute. Unpublished.

Langenberg, Donald N. 1997. Diplomas and degrees are obsolescent. *Chronicle of Higher Education*, 12 September, A64.

Leavitt, Michael. 1997. A learning enterprise for the cybercentury: The Western Governors University. In *The Learning Revolution*, edited by Diana Oblinger and Sean Rush. Bolton, Mass.: Anker Publishing Company, 180–94.

Lenn, Marjorie Peace. 1997. The global alliance for transnational education: Transnational education and the quality imperative. Proceedings of the EUNIS 97 Conference, 9–11 September, Grenoble, France.

Lewis, Ted. 1996. Surviving the software economy. *Upside Magazine* (March). <http://www.upside.com/texis/mvm/story?id=34712c1256>.

McMasters, John H., and Lee A. Matsch. 1996. Desired attributes of an engineering graduate: An industry perspective. 19th American Institute of Aeronautics and Astronautics Advanced Measurement and Ground Testing Technology Conference, 17–20 June, New Orleans.

McPherson, Michael S., and Morton Schapiro. 1996. Are we keeping college affordable? Student aid, access, and choice in American higher education. Stanford Forum for Higher Education, 16–18 October.

Marks, Joseph L. 1996. *SREB Fact Book on Higher Education* (1994/1995). Atlanta: Southern Regional Education Board.

Massy, William F. 1997. Life on the wired campus: How information technology will shape institutional futures. In *The Learning Revolution*, edited by Diana Oblinger and Sean Rush. Bolton, Mass.: Anker Publishing Company, 195–210.

Mayadas, Frank. 1997. Asynchronous learning networks. In *The Learning Revolution*, edited by Diana Oblinger and Sean Rush. Bolton, Mass.: Anker Publishing, 211–30.

Menand, Louis. 1997. Everybody else's college education. *New York Times Magazine* (20 April): 48–49.

Merryfield, Merry. 1995. Teacher education in global and international education. *ERIC Digest* online (July).

Miller, Berna. 1997. The quest for lifelong learning: American demographics, March. <http://marketingtools.com/Publications/AD/97_ad/9703_ad/AD97037.htm>.

Miller, Margaret A. 1995. Technoliteracy and the new professor. *New Literary History* 26 (3): 601–12.

Mooney, Carolyn J. 1989. End of mandatory retirement not expected to affect teaching. *Chronicle of Higher Education*, 4 October, A17.

Mosle, Sara. 1997. Public education's last, best chance. *New York Times Magazine* (31 August): 30–33, 36–37, 48–50, 55–56, 60–61.

Munitz, Barry. 1995. Managing transformation in an age of social triage. In *Reinventing the University: Managing and Financing Institutions of Higher Education*, edited by Sandra L. Johnson and Sean C. Rush. New York: John Wiley & Sons, Inc., 21–48.

A Nation at Risk. 1983. <http://www.ed.gov/pubs/NatAtRisk/risk.html>.

National Association of Business (NAB). 1997a. Teens want to be pushed in school—but many still don't see the relevance. *Work America* 14, no. 4 (April): 6.

———. 1997b. Executives agree: National standards would improve schools. *Work America* 14, no. 5 (May): 2.

———. 1997c. <http://www.nab.com/econ/studies.html#creation>.

———. 1997d. Paper from Business Policy Council for Workforce Development, 21 May.

———. 1997e. The multifaceted returns to education. <http://www.nab.com/econ/returntoed.html>.

National Association of Business Economists. 1996. Industry survey.

Noam, Eli M. 1995. Electronics and the dim future of the university. *Science* 270 (13 October): 247–49.

———. 1997. Electronics and the dim future of academic publishers. Forum for the Future of Higher Education, 21–23 September.

Oblinger, Diana, Jim Mingle, and Mark Resmer. 1998. Student mobile computing. In *The Future Compatible Campus*, edited by Diana Oblinger and Sean Rush. Bolton, Mass.: Anker Publishing, 88–108.

Porter, Michael. 1985. *Competitive Advantage: Creating and Sustaining Superior Performance*. New York: Free Press.

Potter, Edward E., and Judith A. Youngman. 1997. Keeping America competitive: Employment policy for the twenty-first century. <http://www.epfnet.org/epf/keep.htm>.

Prusak, Laurence. 1997a. The changing nature of work. IBM Corporation. Unpublished.

———. 1997b. Introduction to knowledge in organizations. In *Knowledge in Organizations*, edited by Laurence Prusak. Boston: Butterworth-Heinemann Publishing, ix–xv.

Reese, Shelly. 1996. Illiteracy at work. *American Demographics* (April). <http://www.marketingtool..._AD/9604AB02.htm>.

Reich, Robert. 1991. *The Work of Nations: Preparing Ourselves for 21ˢᵗ Century Capitalism*. New York: A.A. Knopf.

———. 1996. The seven new directions at work. Fourth Annual Address on the State of the American Workforce, Center for National Policy, 3 September. <http://www.dol.gov/dol/_...media/speeches.seven.htm>.

Resmer, Mark, James R. Mingle, and Diana G. Oblinger. 1995. *Computers for All Students: A Strategy for Universal Access to Information Resources.* Denver: State Higher Education Executive Officers (SHEEO).

Rigden, Diana. 1996. What business leaders can do to help change teacher education. Washington: American Association of Colleges for Teacher Education.

Sivin-Kachala, Jay, and Ellen Bialo. 1994. Report on the effectiveness of technology in schools 1990–1994. Washington: Software Publishers Association.

Smith, Thomas M. 1996. The pocket condition of education 1996. NCES 96–305. U.S. Department of Education, National Center for Education Statistics, Washington.

Software Publishers Association. 1997. *SPA Education Market Report, Second Printing.* Washington: Software Publishers Association.

Speer, Tibett L. 1996. A nation of students. *American Demographics* (August). <http://www.marketingtool..._AD/9608AF02.htm>.

Sperling, John, and Tucker, Robert W. 1997. Time for natinally authorized universities. *The NLII Viewpoint* 2, no. 1 (fall): 50–60.

Sternberg, Robert, J. 1996. *Successful Intelligence.* New York: Simon and Schuster.

Tate, R. Grant. 1995. At the crossroad: Higher education and technology development. *Technos* 4, no. 4 (winter): 26–30.

Trachtenberg, Stephen Joel. 1997. Older students will bring new opportunities to colleges. *Chronicle of Higher Education,* 21 March, B7.

Twigg, Carol. 1997. Notes on creating and delivering collegiate learning materials in a distributed (networked) learning environment: A business model for university-corporate collaboration. Unpublished.

Twigg, Carol, and Robert Heterick. 1997. The NLII vision: Implications for systems and states. Working Paper for NLII-SHEEO Seminar on the Public Policy Implications of the Information Technology Revolution, 13–14 November, Denver.

Twigg, Carol, and Diana Oblinger. 1997. *The Virtual University.* Washington: Educom.

UNESCO. 1996. Learning without frontiers and the Amman affirmation. <http://www.education/unesco/educprog/lwf/index.html>.

United States National Research Center. 1996. Mathematics and science curriculum and standards: An international comparison. Third international mathematics and science study. 1996 National Education Summit. Unpublished.

University Continuing Education Association. 1992. *Lifelong Learning Trends: A Profile of Continuing Higher Education, Second Edition.* Washington: University Continuing Education Association.

Van Alstyne, Marshall. 1996. Applying a theory of information and technology to higher education. Presentation at Stanford Forum for Higher Education, 16–18 October.

Verville, Anne-Lee. 1995. What business needs from higher education. *Educational Record* 76(4): 46–50.

———. 1996. Workplace trends and human resource needs: What business wants from higher education. American Council on Education 78th Annual Meeting, 20 February, San Diego.

———. 1997. Living in the information society: Achieving education equity with advanced technology. IBM Policy Series. <http://www.ibm.com/ibm/publicaffairs/access/index.html>.

Waterman, R. 1994. Frontiers of excellence—learning from companies that put people first. London: Brealey.

Wilson, Jack. 1997. Reengineering the undergraduate curriculum. In *The Learning Revolution,* edited by Diana Oblinger and Sean Rush. Bolton, Mass.: Anker Publishing Company, 107–28.

Wingspread Group on Higher Education. 1993. *An American Imperative: Higher Expectations for Higher Education.* Racine, Wisc.: The Johnson Foundation, Inc.

Wulf, W. A. 1995. Warning: Information technology will transform the university. *Issues in Science and Technology* (summer): 46–53.

INDEX

by Linda Webster

Certification, 108–9, 139
Change. *See also* Globalization
  accelerated rate of, 15, 155
  challenges of generally, v–xi
  challenging paradigm paralysis, 158–59
  comfort with, 155–56, 163
  complacency and, 160, 162
  compound growth and, 162–63
  culture of, 159–62
  demographic changes in workforce, 5–7
  fixed culture and, 161
  information technology as change
    agent, 43–54
  and lack of vision, 160
  leadership and, 87, 162–64
  lifelong learning and, 162–63
  obstacles to, 161
  poor communication and, 160–61
  and preparation for tomorrow, 156–57
  reasons for failure of, 160–61
  summary of needed changes in higher
    education, 156–57
  support for, 161–62
  and thinking in future tense, 155–57
  transformative agents and, 75–77
Chemical Abstracts Society, 89
Chickering, Arthur W., 104–5
Chile, 56
China, 41, 56
Clendenin, John, 120
Coaching, 14
Coley, Richard, 120
Collaborative learning, 106–7
College graduates. *See also* Higher
    education; Workforce
  benefits of degree for, 21–24
  complaints about higher education by,
    23, 94, 107, 148
  deficiencies of, from business perspec-
    tive, 4, 22–23
  degrees conferred on, 35–36
  earnings of, 24
  fields of study by, 36
  flexibility of, 23–24
  job interviews and, 91
  personal development of, 21
  work preparation for, 21–23

College students. *See also* Higher
    education; Learning environment
  age of, 34–35
  characteristics of, 31–38
  computers owned by, 135
  degrees conferred on, 35–36
  distribution of learners, 31–38
  failure rate of, 32–33
  female versus male students, 35
  fields of study by, 36
  learning environment for, 94–109
  lower income students and rising costs,
    37–38
  minority students, 35
  part-time versus full-time students, 33
  projected growth in enrollments, 33–34
  in proprietary institutions, 34
  in public versus private institutions,
    33–34
  tuition and fee increases for, 33, 36–38
  in two-year institutions, 34
Colleges. *See* Higher education; and
    specific colleges
Colorado Department of Labor, 48
Columbia Pictures, 60
"Comfort zone," 163
Communication and change, 160–61
Communication skills, 22, 74, 80–81
Community colleges
  enrollments concentrated in relatively
    few academic areas, 34
  failure rate for students in, 33
  growth in enrollments in, 34
  tuition and fees at, 36–37
Competitive advantage
  factors in, 146
  global competition and, 58–60
  higher education and, 146–47
  knowledge and, v–vii
Complacency, 160, 162
Complexity of work, 9–14
Compound growth, 162–63
Computer-generated music and art, 52
Computer ownership, 135
Computers in the home, 39
Computing. *See* Information technology
    (IT); Networks
Confederation of British Industry, 20

security and, 16–18, 62
and skilled versus unskilled worker
  shortages, 112
and skills for flexible organization, 74–
  77
statistics on job changes, 16
and successful intelligence, 71–74,
  127–28
teamwork and, 14–15, 22, 74, 81–83
telecommuting or working from home
  offices, 14
traditional versus high-performance
  work, 75
transformative agents in, 75–77
and world of work and corporate
  culture, 77
Workplace. *See also* Business; Workforce
ambiguity in, 13, 22
benefits of college degree in, 21–24
and change at accelerated rate, 15
creativity in, 86–87
demands of, 77–78
fidelity between education and work,
  126–28
globalization and, 12–13
growing complexity of work, 9–14
individual mobility in, 14–15
and intangible outcomes for businesses,
  9–10
job mobility in, 14, 26
job security in, 17–18

knowledge emphasized in, 10–11
leadership in, 87–88
and mergers, alliances, and new
  companies, 12
mobility in, 14–15
multiple management styles in, 13–14
new rules for, 4–5
outsourcing and, 15, 17, 62
physical mobility in, 14
problem solving and decision making
  in, 84–86, 127–28
productivity and, 15–16
project management in, 88–89
ratio of cerebral to manual work, 19
reduced supervision in, 13
security and, 16–18, 62
teamwork in, 14–15, 22, 74, 81–83
traditional versus high-performance
  work, 75
and world of work and corporate
  culture, 77
World Wide Web (WWW), 49–50, 52,
  80, 89, 99
Written communication, 80
Wulf, W. A., 24

Youngman, Judith A., 18, 56, 58, 62